1

Life

SECOND EDITION

**NATIONAL
GEOGRAPHIC**
L E A R N I N G

HELEN STEPHENSON

JOHN HUGHES

PAUL DUMMETT

Australia · Brazil · Mexico · Singapore · United Kingdom · United States

Contents

Pronunciation	Listening	Reading	Speaking	Writing
word stress questions	introductions phone numbers	a description of two people an article about international phone calls from New York	introductions a quiz greeting people	text type: an identification card writing skill: capital letters
we're, they're *I'm, isn't, aren't* *be*: questions and short answers plural nouns syllables	a description of a place a conversation about a vacation	a description of photos of a trip a conversation about a vacation a quiz about vacation spots	vacation photos on vacation general knowledge	text type: a form writing skill: capital letters
possessive *'s* linking with *in* intonation	a description of a family from Mexico a conversation about a family from Iraq a description of good friends	a description of a family from Scotland an article about important days	my family people and things celebrations around the world	text type: a greeting card writing skill: contractions
th /ð/ linking with *can*	a description of Astana tourist information	a description of places in a town a description of two famous towers an article about time zones	locations famous places days and times	text type: a text message writing skill: *and*
can/can't *have/has* numbers	a profile of Yves Rossy an interview with a robot expert people talk about their interesting possessions	an article about robots and people a blog post about gadgets	my abilities my things my favorite piece of technology	text type: an email writing skill: *but*
do you ...? *likes, doesn't like* intonation	a description of a sport in South Africa an interview with a man about sports	an article about a sport a profile of a TV presenter an article about street food	sports interests food	text type: short messages writing skill: punctuation and sentence structure

Pronunciation	Listening	Reading	Speaking	Writing
intonation in questions sentence stress	a description of the Holi festival interviews about hobbies with friends	an article about a day in China an article about the seasons in British Columbia	my partner and I a survey about hobbies my favorite season	text type: a profile writing skill: paragraphs
-s and -es verb endings /s/ and /z/	an interview about a man's job an interview about an unusual school	an article about jobs on the London Underground an article about a job in a wildlife park	jobs things we usually do	text type: an email writing skill: spelling: double letters
there are I'd like, We'd like	four people talk about travel a conversation about a trip to Cape Town	an article about things in people's suitcases an article about a trans-Siberian trip	things in my suitcase hotels and tourist places travel tips	text type: travel advice writing skill: because
was/were weak forms sentence stress	a profile of Ayrton Senna a radio program about people we remember	a quiz about "firsts" in exploration an article about the first people in the American continents	dates and events people in my past who was he/she?	text type: an email writing skill: expressions in emails
-ed regular simple past verbs did you …? didn't	old books and documents in Timbuktu an interview with a woman from New Orleans	an article about an unusual discovery a story about an adventure in Madagascar	did it happen? last week and last year one day last week	text type: a life story writing skill: when
going and doing would you …?	three people talk about weekend activities a description of a family in Indonesia	a short message about next weekend an article about helping people on weekends	my photos next weekend a special weekend	text type: a thank you note writing skill: spelling: verb endings

Life around the world—in 12 videos

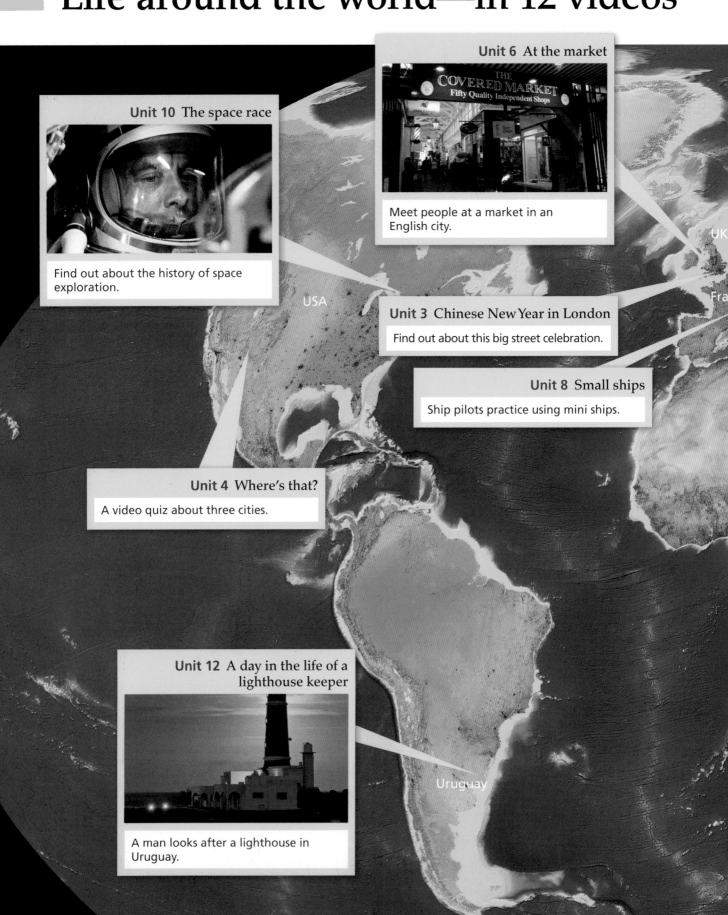

Unit 10 The space race

Find out about the history of space exploration.

Unit 6 At the market

Meet people at a market in an English city.

USA

UK

Fran

Unit 3 Chinese New Year in London

Find out about this big street celebration.

Unit 8 Small ships

Ship pilots practice using mini ships.

Unit 4 Where's that?

A video quiz about three cities.

Unit 12 A day in the life of a lighthouse keeper

A man looks after a lighthouse in Uruguay.

Uruguay

Unit 9 The people of the reindeer

Find out about the lives of the Sami people.

Unit 11 True stories?

Three people tell their stories. Are they true or false?

Russia

Unit 5 What's your favorite gadget?

Two people talk about their favorite gadgets.

Nepal

Unit 1 My top ten photos

A photographer talks about his favorite photos.

Kenya

Australia

Unit 7 The elephants of Samburu

Find out about elephants in the Samburu National Park.

Unit 2 A vacation in Australia

On vacation with two friends.

**UNIT 1
HELLO**

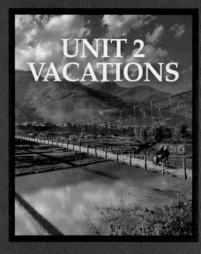

**UNIT 2
VACATIONS**

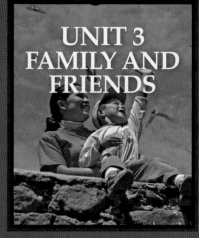

**UNIT 3
FAMILY AND
FRIENDS**

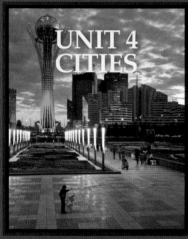

**UNIT 4
CITIES**

**UNIT 5
MY THINGS**

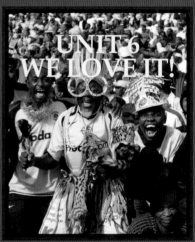

**UNIT 6
WE LOVE IT!**

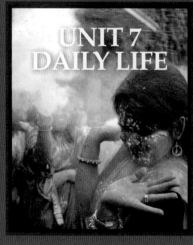

**UNIT 7
DAILY LIFE**

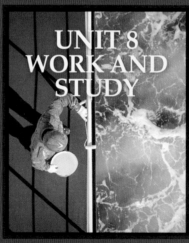

**UNIT 8
WORK AND
STUDY**

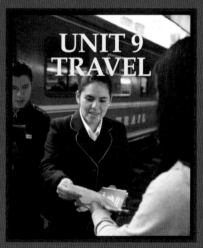

**UNIT 9
TRAVEL**

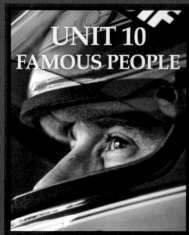

**UNIT 10
FAMOUS PEOPLE**

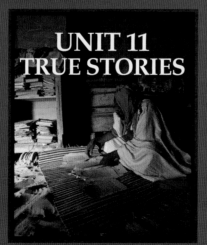

**UNIT 11
TRUE STORIES**

**UNIT 12
THE WEEKEND**

David Doubilet in the
Pacific Ocean, Australia

FEATURES

1 ▶1 Look at the photo. Listen and read.

Hello! I'm David.

2 ▶1 Listen again and repeat.

3 Say your name.

Hello! I'm _____ .

4 Work in pairs.

Hello! I'm Dani.

Hello! I'm Lee.

1a People

Listening

1 ▶2 Listen and read.

1
D: Hello. I'm David.
M: Hi. I'm Mireya.
D: Mireya Mayor?
M: Yes.

2
D: Hi! I'm David Doubilet.
M: Hello.
D: Oh! You're Mireya!
M: Yes. I'm Mireya Mayor.

3
D: Hello. I'm David Doubilet.
M: I'm Mireya.
D: Mireya?
M: Yes. M–I–R–E–Y–A.
D: Hi. Nice to meet you.

NATIONAL GEOGRAPHIC PEOPLE

David Doubilet

Mireya Mayor

Vocabulary the alphabet

2 ▶ 3 Listen and repeat.

Aa	Bb	Cc	Dd	Ee	Ff	Gg
Hh	Ii	Jj	Kk	Ll	Mm	Nn
Oo	Pp	Qq	Rr	Ss	Tt	Uu
Vv	Ww	Xx	Yy	Zz

3 ▶ 4 Say the letters. Listen. Write the letters.

A	B	L	I	O	Q	R
H	C					
	D					

4 ▶ 5 Listen and repeat.

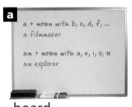
board

book

chair

desk

door

window

5 Work in pairs.
Student A: Say the letters.
Student B: Say the word.

C–H–A–I–R

Chair.

Yes!

6 ▶ 6 Listen. Write the names.

1 _____
2 _____
3 _____
4 _____

7 Work in pairs.
Student A: Spell your name.
Student B: Write the name.

Grammar *be*: *I + am, you + are*

▶ **BE: I + AM, YOU + ARE**

| I'm | David. |
| You're | Mireya. |

(I'm = I am, You're = You are)

Now look at page 158.

8 Write *I* or *You*.

S: Hello. _____ 'm Sandra.
K: Hi!
S: Oh! _____ 're Kim!
K: Yes, _____ 'm Kim Smith.

Speaking *my*Life

9 ▶ 7 Listen and read. Speak to other students.

Hi, I'm Carlos.

Hello. I'm Sonia. Nice to meet you, Carlos.

Nice to meet you, Sonia.

1b People and places

1 This is Jane. She's from Buenos Aires. It's in Argentina. Jane is Argentinian.

2 This is Lukas. He's from Cape Town. It's in South Africa. Lukas is South African.

Reading

1 ▶ 8 Read and listen.

2 Write the words in the chart.

	Photo 1	Photo 2
Name	Jane	
Country		
Nationality		South African

Vocabulary countries and nationalities

3 ▶ 9 Write the words in the chart. Listen and check.

Egyptian	Mexico
Spanish	the United States

	Country	Nationality
1	Brazil	Brazilian
2	Egypt	_____
3	Italy	Italian
4	_____	Mexican
5	Spain	_____
6	the United Kingdom	British
7	_____	American
8	Vietnam	Vietnamese

4 Pronunciation word stress

▶ 10 Listen and repeat the countries. Copy the stress.

• ●   ● • •
Brazil   Mexico

Grammar *be: he/she/it + is*

▶ **BE: HE/SHE/IT + IS**

He		from Russia.
She	**is**	Russian.
It		in Russia.

(He's, She's, It's = He is, She is, It is)

Now look at page 158.

5 Look at the photos. Write *He's, She's,* or *It's.*

1 Tran

2 Juan

3 Krishnan

4 Marina

1 Tran is from Hanoi. _____ in Vietnam. _____ Vietnamese.
2 Juan is from Santiago. _____ in Chile. _____ Chilean.
3 Krishnan is from Chicago. _____ in the United States. _____ American.
4 Marina is from Milan. _____ in Italy. _____ Italian.

6 Write your information. Show your partner.

	You
Name	
City	
Country	
Nationality	

7 Tell the class about your partner.

Kira is from Paris. It's in France. She's French.

Vocabulary numbers 1–10

8 ▶ 11 Write the numbers (1–10). Listen and repeat.

_0_ zero	____ four	____ eight
____ one	____ five	____ nine
____ two	____ six	____ ten
____ three	____ seven	

9 ▶ 12 Look at the chart in Exercise 3. Listen. Say the country.

"five" *Spain*

10 ▶ 13 Look at the chart in Exercise 3. Listen. Say the number.

"Spain" *five*

Speaking *my* Life

11 ▶ 14 Work in pairs. Take the quiz. Are the sentences true (T) or false (F)? Listen and check.

Baseball is Russian.

False. It's American.

QUIZ TRUE OR FALSE?

around the world

F

01 Baseball is Russian.

02 Pasta is from South Africa.

03 Jaguar is British.

04 Flamenco is from Italy.

12 Work in pairs. Write an *around the world* quiz. Write four sentences. Test the class.

1c Phone calls from New York

Reading

1 Read *Phone calls from New York* on page 15. <u>Underline</u> four countries.

2 Read again. Write the names.

1 _____ is a teacher.
2 _____ is Mexican.
3 _____ is from Canada.
4 _____ is Indian.

Listening

3 ▶ **15** Listen to Anne-Marie. Circle the phone number (a or b).

a 555 730 7121   b 555 760 7101

4 ▶ **16** Listen to Nelson. Write.

1 work phone number _____
2 home phone number _____

Grammar *my, your*

> ▶ **MY, YOUR**
>
> *What's **your** phone number?*
> ***My** phone number is 555 760 7101.*

Now look at page 158.

5 Write *my* or *your*.
R: Hi. ¹_____ name's Ramon.
N: Hello. I'm Nelson.
...
N: Ramon, what's ²_____ phone number?
R: ³_____ work number is 555 275 6975.
N: What's ⁴_____ cell phone number?
R: It's 555 398 9763.

6 Work in pairs. Ask and answer questions. Write your partner's:
home number   _____
cell phone number   _____

Vocabulary greetings

7 ▶ **17** Write the expressions in the correct places. Listen and repeat.

Bye	Hello

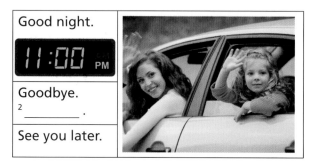

Hi.
¹_____ .

09:00 AM
Good morning.

02:00 PM
Good afternoon.

07:00 PM
Good evening.

Good night.
11:00 PM

Goodbye.
²_____ .

See you later.

Critical thinking greetings

8 *Good evening* and *good night* have different meanings. Circle the correct greetings.

1 A: Hello.
   B: *Good evening.* / *Good night.* How are you?
2 A: *Good evening.* / *Good night.*
   B: Goodbye! See you tomorrow!

Which greeting means "hello"? Which greeting means "goodbye"?

Speaking *my*Life

9 Practice the conversations in Exercise 8 with your classmates.

PHONE CALLS FROM NEW YORK: THE TOP TEN COUNTRIES

▶ 18

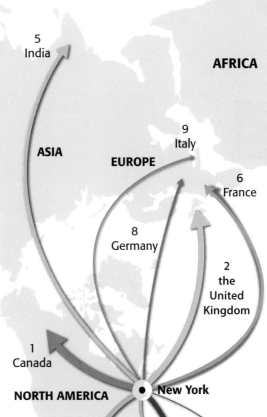

AUSTRALIA

5
India

AFRICA

ASIA

9
Italy

EUROPE

6
France

8
Germany

2
the
United
Kingdom

1
Canada

New York

NORTH AMERICA

4
Mexico

7
Jamaica

3
Dominican
Republic

10
Brazil

SOUTH AMERICA

My name's Nina. I'm a student. I'm in New York. My family is in India. I'm Indian.

My name's Anne-Marie. I'm in New York. I'm a student. I'm Canadian. My family is in Canada.

My name's Ramon. I'm a doctor. I'm in New York. I'm Mexican. My family is in Mexico.

My name's Nelson. I'm Brazilian. I'm a teacher. I'm in New York. My family is in Brazil.

1d What's this in English?

Vocabulary in the classroom

1 ▶ 19 Listen. Write the words.

1

2

_____   _____

3

4

_____   _____

5

6

_____   _____

7

8

_____   _____

2 ▶ 20 Listen to the words from Exercise 1 and repeat.

3 Work in pairs. Point to a photo in Exercise 1. Ask and answer questions.

> What's this in English?

> It's a _____ .

> Can you spell it?

> Yes. _____ .

Real life classroom language

4 ▶ 21 Listen. Look at the classroom language box.

5 ▶ 21 Listen again. Who says each expression? Write T (teacher) or S (student).

▶ CLASSROOM LANGUAGE

Good afternoon, everyone. _T_
Sit down, please. ___
Open your books. ___
Look at page six. ___
Sorry I'm late. ___
Can you repeat that, please? ___
I don't understand. ___
Can you spell it, please? ___
What's this in English? ___
Do Exercise 7 at home. ___
See you next time. ___

6 Pronunciation questions

a ▶ 22 Listen and repeat the questions from the classroom language box.

b Look at track 21 of the audioscript on page 182. Practice conversations 4, 6, and 7.

7 Work in pairs. Write the words. Practice the conversations.

1   T: Good morning. _____ I'm late.
    S: That's OK. Sit down, _____ .

2   S: Can you _____ that, please?
    T: Yes. Look at _____ ten.

1e My ID

Writing an identification card

1 Look at the ID card. Circle the name of the company and the name of the visitor.

2 Writing skill capital letters

a <u>Underline</u> on the ID card the capital letters in the names of the company, place, and visitor.

b Write these words in the chart.

Brazil	Portuguese	Rio de Janeiro
Brazilian	Nelson Pires	

a name	Dan Pillsbury _____
a city	Boston _____
a country	the United States _____
a nationality	American _____
a language	English _____

c Circle the letters that should be capital letters.

1 santiago is in chile.
2 maya davis is a teacher.
3 I'm chinese.
4 I speak french.

3 Complete the ID cards with the information. Use capital letters.

1 dublin
sean booth

2 american
cathy

3 bangkok
laura davis

4 Write your own ID card.

5 Work in pairs. Check your partner's card. Check the capital letters.

A woman and a baby from Nepal

Before you watch

1 Work in pairs. Look at this photo. Complete the information about Tom.

I'm	is	my	name's

Hi. My ¹ _____ Tom. ² _____ a photographer. This ³ _____ my top ten— ⁴ _____ favorite *National Geographic* photos of people and places.

While you watch

2 ▭◀1 Watch the video. Check (✓) the correct columns.

photo	a man	a woman	people	an animal/ animals
1				
2				
3				
4				
5				
6				
7				
8				
9				
10				

3 Work in pairs. Compare your answers from Exercise 2.

Photo number two is a man.

Yes, I agree.

4 ▭◀1 Watch the video again. Circle the correct country.
Photo 1   Nepal / India
Photo 2   Nepal / Mongolia
Photo 3   Mongolia / China
Photo 4   the United States / Canada
Photo 5   Brazil / Bangladesh
Photo 6   Canada / New Zealand
Photo 7   Australia / the United States
Photo 8   South Africa / Mozambique
Photo 9   Namibia / Kenya
Photo 10 Kenya / South Africa

5 ▭◀1 Read the sentences. Are the sentences true (T) or false (F)? Watch the video again and check.

Photo 2	The man is from the Himalayas.	T	F
Photo 3	The woman is happy.	T	F
Photo 7	The climber is Jimmy Chin.	T	F
Photo 8	The woman is from Namibia.	T	F
Photo 10	Tom says, "It's my favorite."	T	F

6 ▭◀1 Watch the video again. Work in pairs. What's your favorite photo?

After you watch

7 Complete the information about three of the photos.

Photo 1 is by Alex Treadway. The woman is ¹ _____ Nepal in the Himalayas. ² _____ Nepalese.

Photo 7 ³ _____ by Jimmy Chin. This ⁴ _____ Kate Rutherford. ⁵ _____'s an American climber.

Photo 9 is of people ⁶ _____ Namibia. ⁷ _____ by Chris Johns. ⁸ _____ a *National Geographic* photographer.

8 Write about your favorite photo.

UNIT 1 REVIEW AND MEMORY BOOSTER

Grammar

1 Complete the sentences with these words.

I'm	you're	it's	he's	she's

1 My name's Rosa. _____ from Brazil.
2 This is David. _____ a teacher.
3 I'm from Ottawa. _____ in Canada.
4 A: I'm Alain.
   B: Oh! _____ my teacher!
5 Marina is from Italy. _____ Italian.

2 Complete the sentences with *my* or *your*.

1 I'm Susana. What's _____ name?
2 Hello. I'm _____ teacher.
3 Hi. _____ name's Samir.
4 What's _____ phone number?
5 Open _____ books to page four.

3 **>> MB** Make true sentences.

My name's _____ . I'm from _____ .
I'm _____ .

I CAN
talk about people and places (*be*)
use *my* and *your* correctly
greet people

Vocabulary

4 Write the names of the objects.

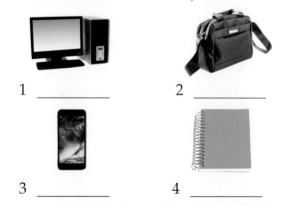

1 _____   2 _____

3 _____   4 _____

5 Complete the countries. Write the nationalities.

1 V _ _ t n _ m   _____
2 _ g _ p t   _____
3 S _ _ t h _ f r _ c _   _____
4 R _ s s _ _   _____
5 B r _ z _ l   _____

6 **>> MB** Work in pairs. Take turns.
Student A: Write five numbers. Say the numbers to your partner.
Student B: Write the numbers. Check.

7 **>> MB** Work in pairs. Take turns.
Student A: Write five words. Say the letters of the words to your partner.
Student B: Write the words. Check.

I CAN
talk about things in the classroom
talk about countries and nationalities
count to ten
say the alphabet and spell words

Real life

8 Match 1–4 with a–d to make exchanges.

1 Sorry I'm late. ___
2 What's this in English? ___
3 This is a table. ___
4 Can you repeat that, please? ___

a Yes. *Work in pairs.*
b Can you spell it, please?
c It's a computer.
d That's OK. Sit down, please.

9 Work in pairs. Practice the exchanges in Exercise 8.

I CAN
understand classroom instructions
talk to my teacher and my classmates about the lesson

Unit 2 Vacations

Two people on a bridge in Mai Chau

FEATURES

1 ▶ 23 Look at the photo. Circle the correct option (a or b). Listen and check.

a This is in France. It's a city. It's night.
b This is in Vietnam. It's a river. It's morning.

2 ▶ 24 Look at these two places. Listen and repeat.

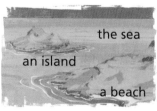

3 Complete the sentences with words from Exercise 2.

1 Bangkok is _____ . It's in Thailand.
2 Titicaca is _____ . It's in Bolivia and Peru.
3 Everest is _____ . It's in China and Nepal.

4 Work in pairs. Write four sentences about places. Read your sentences to your partner.

21

2a My vacation

MY VACATION BLOG by Laura ▶ 26

THURSDAY
03 JAN

Today is Thursday. I'm in Tunisia. It's beautiful! It's evening. I'm with my friends Brad, Andy, and Jessica. We're on a beach. We're happy. Andy and Jessica are Canadian. They're doctors. They're on vacation, too.

Vocabulary **days of the week**

1 ▶ 25 Number the days of the week in order (1–7). Listen, check, and repeat.

_1_ Monday   ___ Saturday
___ Sunday   ___ Wednesday
___ Friday   ___ Thursday
___ Tuesday

2 Work in pairs.
Student A: Say a day.
Student B: Say the next day.

Reading

3 Work in pairs. Look at the photo. Circle the place.

a   a city   b   a beach

4 Work in pairs. Read *My vacation blog*. Find:

1   the day of the week
2   the name of the country
3   the names of the people

Grammar *be: we/they + are*

▶ **BE: WE/THEY + ARE**

We They	are	in Tunisia. Canadian.

(We're, They're = We are, They are)

Now look at page 160.

5 Look at the grammar box. <u>Underline</u> *we're* and *they're* in *My vacation blog*.

6 ▶ 27 Complete the sentences. Listen and check.

1   This is Jane. This is Paul. They_____ Australian.
2   I'm Meera. This is Suri. We_____ from India.
3   In this photo, I'm with my friend Jack. _____'re in Egypt.
4   Laura is with Brad, Andy, and Jessica. _____ on vacation.

7 Pronunciation *we're, they're*

a ▶ 28 Listen and repeat the sentences from Exercise 6.

b Work in pairs. Write sentences with *We're*. Read your sentences to a new pair.

Grammar *be*: negative forms

▶ BE: NEGATIVE FORMS

I You	am not ('m not) are not (aren't)	
He/She/It	is not (isn't)	happy. on a beach.
We/You/They	are not (aren't)	

Now look at page 160.

8 Work in pairs. Look at the grammar box. What are the negative forms of *am, is,* and *are*?

9 Work in pairs. Correct the false sentences about the photo on page 22.

1 It's Wednesday.
 It isn't Wednesday. It's Thursday.
2 The friends are in a city.
3 It's morning.
4 They're sad.
5 Andy and Jessica are from Tunisia.

10 Look at the photo for Saturday. Write these words in the blog post.

not	aren't	isn't	isn't

11 Pronunciation *I'm, isn't, aren't*

a ▶ 29 Listen and repeat the sentences.

b Work in pairs. Write true sentences. Read your sentences to your partner.

> *We aren't on a beach.*

I'm I'm not You're You aren't We're We aren't	a student. a doctor. in a city. in a classroom. in Egypt. happy. on a lake. on a beach. on vacation. from Morocco.

Speaking **my Life**

12 Work in groups. Show a photo to your group. Tell your group about your photo. Use affirmative and negative forms of *be*.

> *This is a photo of my friends, Carlos and Enrique. They're in Egypt. They aren't happy.*

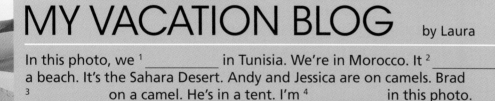

MY VACATION BLOG by Laura

SATURDAY JAN 05

In this photo, we ¹_____ in Tunisia. We're in Morocco. It ²_____ a beach. It's the Sahara Desert. Andy and Jessica are on camels. Brad ³_____ on a camel. He's in a tent. I'm ⁴_____ in this photo.

2b Where are you?

Vocabulary numbers 11–100

1 ▶ 30 Write the numbers. Listen and repeat.

_11_	eleven
____	twelve
____	thirteen
____	fourteen
____	fifteen
____	sixteen
____	seventeen
____	eighteen
_19_	nineteen

2 ▶ 31 Write the numbers in order. Listen, check, and repeat.

eighty	fifty	forty
ninety	seventy	sixty
thirty	twenty	

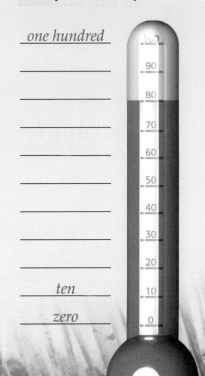

one hundred	100
_____	90
_____	80
_____	70
_____	60
_____	50
_____	40
_____	30
_____	20
ten	10
zero	0

3 ▶ 32 Look at the pictures (a–c). Listen and match.

1 _____   2 _____   3 _____

c City	Temperature
Cape Town	23°C
Casablanca	29°C
Chicago	16°C
Copenhagen	11°C

4 ▶ 33 Look at the numbers in Exercise 3 again. Listen. Are the numbers the same or different?

a "It's thirteen degrees." *different*

5 ▶ 34 Write the numbers. Listen and check.

nineteen	six	thirty-five

1 It's _____ degrees in Seoul today. It's cold.
2 It's _____ degrees in Sydney today. It's hot.
3 It's _____ degrees in Lima today. It's warm.

6 Work in pairs. Look at the cities in Exercise 3. Talk about the temperatures. Use *hot*, *warm*, and *cold*.

It's twenty-three degrees in Cape Town.   *It's warm.*

Reading and listening

7 Lorna is Australian. She's on vacation in Europe. Work in pairs. Read the conversation. Answer the questions.

1 Where's Lorna?

2 Where are Kara and Ona?

3 Where's Greg?

8 ▶ 35 Listen. Circle the correct option.

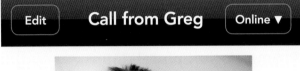

Greg: Hi! Where are you now? Are you in ¹ *France / Italy*?

Lorna: Yes, I am. I'm in the Alps. It's beautiful!

Greg: Are Kara and Ona there, too?

Lorna: No, they aren't. They're on a ² *beach / lake* in Morocco!

Greg: Oh, OK. Is it cold in the Alps?

Lorna: Yes, it is. It's ³ *two / thirty-two* degrees!

Greg: Wow! Are you OK?

Lorna: Yes, I am. I'm in the hotel. It's ⁴ *warm / cold* here.

Greg: That's good. It's ⁵ *thirty-six / sixteen* degrees in Sydney today.

Lorna: Oh! That's ⁶ *hot / cold*!

Grammar *be*: questions and short answers

▶ **BE: QUESTIONS and SHORT ANSWERS**

Am I		Yes, I *am*. No, I'm *not*.
Is she/he/it	OK? cold?	Yes, she/he/it *is*. No, she/he/it *isn't*.
Are we/you/they		Yes, we/you/they *are*. No, we/you/they *aren't*.

Now look at page 160.

9 Look at the grammar box. Look at the conversation in Exercise 8. Read the questions.

10 Write the words in order.

1 you / OK / are / ?
   Are you OK?

2 is / in France / Kara / ?
   _____

3 in Sydney / you and Paul / are / ?
   _____

4 Kara and Ona / in Morocco / are / ?
   _____

5 nice / your hotel / is / ?
   _____

11 Match the questions (1–5) in Exercise 10 with the answers (a–e).

a Yes, they are. ___   d No, she isn't. ___
b Yes, I am. ___   e Yes, we are. ___
c Yes, it is. ___

12 Pronunciation *be*: questions and short answers

▶ 36 Listen and repeat the questions and answers from Exercises 10 and 11.

Speaking *my*Life

13 Work in pairs. You are on vacation. Have a telephone conversation with your friend.
Student A: Turn to page 153.
Student B: Turn to page 155.

2c A vacation quiz

Vocabulary colors

1 ▶ 37 Look at the colors. Listen and repeat.

black　blue　**brown**

green　orange　pink

red　white　yellow

2 Work in pairs. Find six colors in the photos on page 27.

Reading

3 Read the quiz on page 27. Match the photos (a–d) with four of the sentences (1–9).

4 ▶ 38 Look at page 27 again. Listen. Write the words in the box in the correct sentences.

Critical thinking is it always true?

5 Read sentence 1 on page 27. Is this always true? Are all buses in London red? Write the sentences (1–9) on page 27 below.

Always true: _____

Not always true: _____

Grammar *a/an*

▶ A	AN
a + noun with b, c, d, f, … a car	an + noun with a, e, i, o, u an island
Now look at page 160.	

6 Look at the grammar box. Write *a* or *an*.

1 Paris is _____ city.

2 _____ lion is _____ animal.

3 LaGuardia is _____ airport.

Grammar plural nouns

▶ NOUNS	
Singular	**Plural**
an airport	*airports*
a lake	*lakes*
a country	*countries*
a beach	*beaches*
Now look at page 160.	

7 Look at the grammar box. <u>Underline</u> seven plural nouns on page 27.

8 Pronunciation plural nouns

a ▶ 39 Listen and repeat these nouns.

/s/	/z/	/ɪz/
lakes	cars	beaches
airports	countries	buses

b ▶ 40 Write the plural of these nouns. Listen and repeat.

1 a book _____　4 a desk _____

2 a student _____　5 a city _____

3 a dress _____　6 a watch _____

Speaking my Life

9 Work in pairs. Write four sentences—two true and two false. Use these words.

a city / cities	a country / countries
an island / islands	a lake / lakes

Lima and Santiago are cities in Chile.

10 Work in groups. Listen to the sentences. Say *true* or *false*. Correct the false ones.

Lima and Santiago are cities in Chile.

False. Lima is in Peru.

A Vacation Quiz

Australia	black	China
France	island	lakes
Chicago	red	old

1. In London, buses are _____ .
2. In Hawaii, beaches are _____ .
3. Cuba is an _____ .
4. In Cuba, cars are _____ .
5. In Iceland, _____ are hot.
6. Lake Geneva is in two countries—Switzerland and _____ .
7. The Blue Mountains are in _____ .
8. Beijing, Shanghai, and Guangzhou are cities in _____
9. O'Hare is an airport in _____ .

2d Here are your keys

Vocabulary car rental

1 ▶ 41 Listen and match the words (1–4) with the pictures (a–d).

1 a license plate number ___
2 an email address ___
3 an address ___
4 keys ___

b 154 Westwood Avenue Los Angeles CA 90024

c To: jamesp@edu.au

d PT61 APR

2 Work in pairs. Take turns.
Student A: Read an email address.
Student B: Say the number (1–4).

1 smith23@lifemail.com
2 barry@egg.com
3 smnrss@mail.com
4 b.mark@mx.com

3 Work in pairs. Ask your partner for their address and email address.

Real life personal information

4 ▶ 42 Listen to the conversation. Are the sentences true (T) or false (F)?

1 Marta is from Mexico. _____
2 She is on vacation. _____

5 ▶ 42 Listen again. Circle the correct option.

1 Car rental: *two days* / *three days*
2 Name: *Ms. Lopez* / *Mr. Lopez*
3 Email address: *mlopez@daymail.com* / *mlopez@daymail.com.mx*
4 Car license plate number: *UGM 96B* / *UCF 97D*

6 Work in pairs. Look at track 42 of the audioscript on page 183. Practice the conversation.

> ▶ **PERSONAL INFORMATION**
>
> What's your first name/last name?
> Where are you from?
> I'm from Mexico City.
> What's your (email) address/phone number?
> Is this your (email) address/phone number?
> Here's my ID card.
> Here are your keys.
> Note: in email addresses, we say *at* for "@" and *dot* for "."

7 Pronunciation syllables

▶ 43 Listen and repeat the words. Write the number of syllables. <u>Underline</u> the main stress in the words.

vacation   va – <u>ca</u> – tion = 3

1 address ___	4 evening ___	7 seventeen ___
2 car ___	5 key ___	8 telephone ___
3 email ___	6 number ___	

8 Work in pairs. Look at track 42 of the audioscript on page 183. Practice the conversation with new information.

Good evening.

Hello, I'm Mr. Silva.

2e Contact information

Writing a form

1 Match 1 and 2 with the options (a and b).

a a hotel online booking form ____
b an internet profile ____

1

Enya Farrell

User name: enya123

Cell phone: 212-258-0609
Home phone: 212-585-7815
Email address: enya@bt.com
Country: USA
Contacts: 19

2

Title	Ms. ▾
First name	Enya
Last name	Farrell
Address	16 Hampton Road
City	New York
Zip code	10314
Country	USA ▾
Email address	enya@bt.com

2 What's your title? Circle the correct option.

   a Mr.   b Mrs.   c Ms.

3 Writing skill capital letters

a Look at the information in form 2. <u>Underline</u> the capital letters.

b Rewrite this information with the correct capital letters.

   1 11 hill view _____
   2 seattle _____
   3 ryan judd _____
   4 mr. _____

4 Complete the college registration form with the information from Exercise 3b.

🛡 REGISTRATION FORM

Title _____
First name _____
Last name _____
Address _____
City _____
Zip code 98141 _____
Contact number 206-416-9258
Email address ryan@judd.com

5 Complete the online booking form with your own information.

Title	▾
First name	
Last name	
Address	
City	
Zip code	
Country	▾
Email address	

6 Check your form. Check your capital letters.

A koala in a tree in Australia

Before you watch

1 Look at the photo on page 30. What's the animal? Where is it? _____

2 Work in pairs. Look at the map of Australia. Count the states. Answer the questions.

1 Is Brisbane in South Australia?
2 Is Adelaide a city or a state?
3 Is Tasmania an island?

3 Key vocabulary

a Read the sentences. Match the **bold** words (1–4) with the pictures (a–d).

1 **Kangaroos** are from Australia. ___
2 This is **the sun** in the morning. ___
3 **The sky** is blue. ___
4 We're on a **plane**. ___

b ▶ 44 Listen and repeat the **bold** words.

While you watch

4 ◻ 2 Watch the video. Write five words. Read your words to your partner.

water   *blue*

5 ◻ 2 Watch the video again. What order (1–3) do these things appear in the video?

___ sea animals   ___ a city   ___ birds

After you watch

6 Work in pairs. Test your memory. Ask and answer the questions.

1 What animal is in a tree? _____
2 What animal is in the bag? _____
3 What color is the lizard? _____
4 Is the person in the water a man or a woman? _____

7 Work in pairs. Write questions about South Australia with these words.

1 South Australia / beautiful / ?

_____

2 the beaches / nice / ?

_____

3 the animals in South Australia / amazing / ?

_____

4 South Australia / a good place for a vacation / ?

_____

8 Work in pairs. Ask and answer the questions in Exercise 7.

Is South Australia beautiful?

Yes, it is.

No, it isn't.

Grammar

1 Complete the sentences with the words.

'm	isn't	not	we're

GREG: I'm in the mountains. I ¹ _____
with my friends. We're in Canada.
² _____ on vacation. I'm ³ _____
happy—the hotel ⁴ _____ nice.

aren't	isn't	they're	we

KARA: I'm in Brazil with my friends
Jorge and Ana. ⁵ _____ Brazilian. I'm
on vacation. Jorge and Ana ⁶ _____ on
vacation. ⁷ _____'re in Rio de Janeiro.
The water ⁸ _____ cold—it's warm!

2 Work in pairs. Write questions with these
words. Ask and answer the questions.

1 you / a student?
2 your teacher / American?
3 your friends / here?
4 this classroom / cold?
5 we / late for class?

3 ⟫ MB Work in pairs. Look at the words
and write the plurals. Take turns.
Student A: Say a word.
Student B: Say the plural.

1 airport _____   4 city _____
2 beach _____   5 country _____
3 bus _____   6 photo _____

I CAN	
ask and answer questions (*be*)	
use regular plural nouns	

Vocabulary

4 ⟫ MB Work in pairs. Say the days in
order. Take turns. Start with **Monday**.

5 ⟫ MB Work in pairs. Take turns.
Student A: Say a number from 11 to 100.
Student B: Write the number.

6 Circle the correct color.

1 My car is *red / orange.*
2 The buses are *yellow / green.*
3 The lake is *brown / blue.*

I CAN	
say the days of the week	
count from eleven to one hundred	
say the colors of objects	

Real life

7 Complete 1–4 with these words. Then
match 1–4 with a–d.

here's	vacation	name's	this

1 Good afternoon. My _____
  Tanaka.
2 _____ my passport.
3 Are you here on _____?
4 Is _____ your email address?

a Good afternoon, Mr. Tanaka. What's
  your first name please? ___
b No, I'm not. I'm here on business. ___
c Thank you. ___
d Yes, it is. ___

8 Work in pairs. Practice the exchanges in
Exercise 7.

I CAN	
ask for and give personal information	

Unit 3 Family and friends

A family in Mexico looks at butterflies.

FEATURES

1 ▶ **45** Look at the photo. Listen and read.

This family is from Mexico. Rosa is the mother. Lidia is the daughter. Pablo is the son.

2 Write *Lidia*, *Pablo*, and *Rosa*.

1 _____ is a boy.   3 _____ is a girl.

2 _____ is a woman.

3 Write *daughter* and *parents* in the correct place.

father & mother = ¹ _____

son & ² _____ = children

4 Work in pairs. Write sentences about you with a family word. Read your sentences to your partner.

I'm a son.
I'm not a father.

I'm a daughter.
I'm not a mother.

3a Families

▶ 47

The Murray family

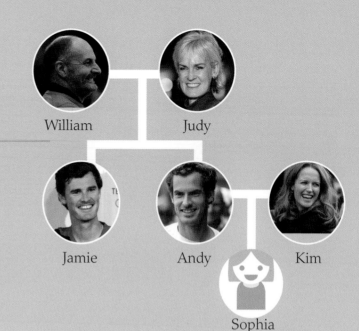

William   Judy

Jamie   Andy   Kim

Sophia

Andy Murray and Jamie Murray are top tennis players. Judy is their mother. She's a tennis player, too. Their father is named William. He isn't a tennis player. Andy is married. His wife is named Kim. Sophia is a little girl. Her parents are Andy and Kim. The Murray family is from Scotland.

Vocabulary family

1 Look at the family tree. Which sport is this family famous for? _____

2 ▶ 46 Listen and repeat the family words.

brother	daughter	father	husband
mother	sister	son	wife

3 Look at the family tree again. Write the correct words.

1 Andy and Jamie are _brothers_ .
2 Andy and Kim are husband and _____ .
3 William and Jamie are father and _____ .
4 Kim and Sophia are mother and _____ .

Reading

4 Read about the Murray family. Write the names.

1 Their parents are William and Judy.
_____ and _____
2 Their sons are Jamie and Andy.
_____ and _____
3 Her mother is Kim.   _____
4 His daughter is Sophia.   _____
5 Her husband is Andy.   _____

Grammar *his, her, its, our, their*

▶ **HIS, HER, ITS, OUR, THEIR**

*He's my father. **His** name's William.*
*She's my mother. **Her** name's Judy.*
*They're my sons. **Their** names are Jamie and Andy.*
***Our** parents are Judy and William.*
*We're from a town in Scotland. **Its** name is Dunblane.*

Now look at page 162.

5 Look at the grammar box. Write *singular* or *plural*.

1 *her* and *his* = _____
2 *our* and *their* = _____

6 Write *her* or *his*.

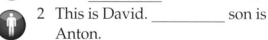

1 This is Sara. _____ mother is Zoe. _____ father is Lucas.
2 This is David. _____ son is Anton.
3 This is Martin. _____ daughters are Mia and Emma.
4 This is Susan. _____ brother is Stephen.
5 This is Andy. _____ parents are William and Judy.

7 Write *our* or *their*.

1 I'm Sam. My brother is Bill. _____ parents are Sue and David.
2 This is a photo of Lili and Jenna. _____ mother is my sister.
3 This is my family. _____ last name is Garcia.
4 This is my sister and her husband. These are _____ children.
5 My brother and his wife are thirty. _____ son is five.

Listening

8 ▶ 48 Look at the photo and the conversation. Write *my, your, his,* or *her*. Listen and check.

A: Is this a photo of ¹ ___your___ family?
B: Yes, it is.
A: Who's this?
B: She's ² _____ sister. ³ _____ name's Heelan. It's her wedding.
A: OK. So is this ⁴ _____ husband?
B: Yes. ⁵ _____ name's Husham.
A: Is this ⁶ _____ daughter?
B: Yes. ⁷ _____ name's Nadia.
A: How old is she?
B: She's twelve years old.

9 Look at the answers. Complete the questions about the people in the photo with these words.

he	she	they	his	her	their

1 Where are _____ ?
   In Baghdad.
2 What's _____ name?
   Nadia.
3 How old is _____ ?
   Twelve years old.
4 What are _____ names?
   Husham and Heelan.
5 What's _____ wife named?
   Heelan.
6 Is _____ the husband?
   No. Husham is the husband.

Speaking myLife

10 Work in pairs. Show your family photos to your partner. Ask and answer questions.

Who's this?

He's my brother.

3b Friends

Ana

Vocabulary people

1 Look at the photo of Ana. Complete the information with four of the words.

| eyes | hair | old | short | tall | young |

My name's Ana. I'm twenty-one years
¹ _____ . My ² _____ are brown and
my ³ _____ is red. I'm not ⁴ _____ .
I'm short. I'm a student at The English
Academy.

2 Work in pairs. Put the words in order to make questions. Answer the questions.

1 color / what / is / hair / your / ?
2 eyes / are / what / your / color / ?
3 are / old / how / you / ?

Listening

3 ▶ 49 Listen to Ana. Match the names (1–3) with the information.

1 Elisa ○   ○ her brother
2 Nuno ○   ○ her classmate
3 Prem ○   ○ her best friend

Elisa

Nuno

4 ▶ 49 Listen again. Complete the sentences.

1 Elisa's eyes are _____ .
2 Elisa's hair is _____ .
3 Nuno's eyes are _____ .
4 Nuno's hair is _____ .
5 Prem's eyes are _____ .
6 Prem's hair is _____ .

5 Work in pairs. Ask and answer questions about three friends. Use the questions in Exercise 2 with *his* or *her*.

My best friends are Luigi, Enzo, and Paulo.

How old is Luigi?

He's 19.

What color are his eyes?

Prem

Grammar possessive 's

> ▶ POSSESSIVE 's
>
> **Ana's** eyes are brown. _____
> **Nuno's** hair is brown. _____
>
> Now look at page 162.

6 Look at the grammar box. Replace the words with the possessive 's with *his* or *her*.

7 Work in pairs. Write sentences with the possessive 's.

1 Ana / Nuno / sister
   Ana is Nuno's sister.
2 Prem / Ana / classmate
3 Ana / eyes / brown
4 Prem / school / The English Academy
5 Ana / friends / Elisa and Prem

8 Pronunciation possessive 's

a ▶ 50 Listen and repeat the sentences from Exercise 7.

b Work in pairs. Make sentences about students in your class.

> *Marco's eyes are brown.*

9 Read the sentences (1–2). Match each 's with its use (a–b).

1 Elisa's my best friend. ____
2 Elisa's eyes are brown. ____

a possessive 's
b contraction of *is*

10 Underline the 's in each sentence. Write P (possessive) or C (contraction).

1 What's this? _____
2 His car's red. _____
3 Jack's books are here. _____
4 Susan and Charlie are my brother's children. _____
5 This is my teacher's book. _____

Speaking my Life

11 Work in pairs. Take turns.
   Student A: Point to a photo. Ask *What's this?*
   Student B: Answer.

> What's this?

> It's Anita's bag.

Anita

Jack

Lin

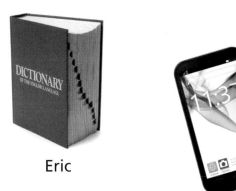

Eric

Claude

Krishnan

12 Work in groups. Ask and answer questions about your things.

3c Important days

Vocabulary months

1 ▶ 51 Number the months in order (1–12). Then listen, check, and repeat.

_1_ January	___ December	___ July
___ April	___ September	___ March
___ October	___ May	___ August
___ June	___ February	___ November

2 Work in pairs. Take turns.
Student A: Say a month.
Student B: Say the number of days.

3 Work in pairs. Complete the sentences.

December	January	October

1 New Year's Day is in _____ .
2 Halloween is in _____ .
3 Christmas Day is in _____ .

Reading

4 Read *Important days*. Match the photos (a and b) with the paragraphs (1–4).

5 Pronunciation **linking with** *in*

▶ 52 Listen and repeat the sentences.

1 It's in March.
2 They're in February.
3 Is it in London?

Critical thinking completing a chart

6 Complete the chart with information from *Important days*.

Grammar irregular plural nouns

> ▶ **IRREGULAR PLURAL NOUNS**
>
> a child → two **children**
> a man → three **men**
> a woman → four **women**
> a person → five **people**

Now look at page 162.

7 Look at the grammar box. Underline the irregular plural nouns in *Important days*.

8 ▶ 53 Listen and repeat the words in the grammar box.

9 ▶ 54 Listen and complete the sentences.

children	men	people	women

1 There are many _____ in Kyle's family.
2 Mark and Peter are _____ .
3 Daniel and David are _____ .
4 Sofia and Camila are _____ .

Writing and speaking

10 Work in pairs. Choose three important words from one of the paragraphs on page 39. Write sentences with your words. Read your sentences to your partner. What's the important day?

American, families, November

> It's American. It's for families. It's in November.

Celebration	Who	Where	When
Chinese New Year			
Thanksgiving			

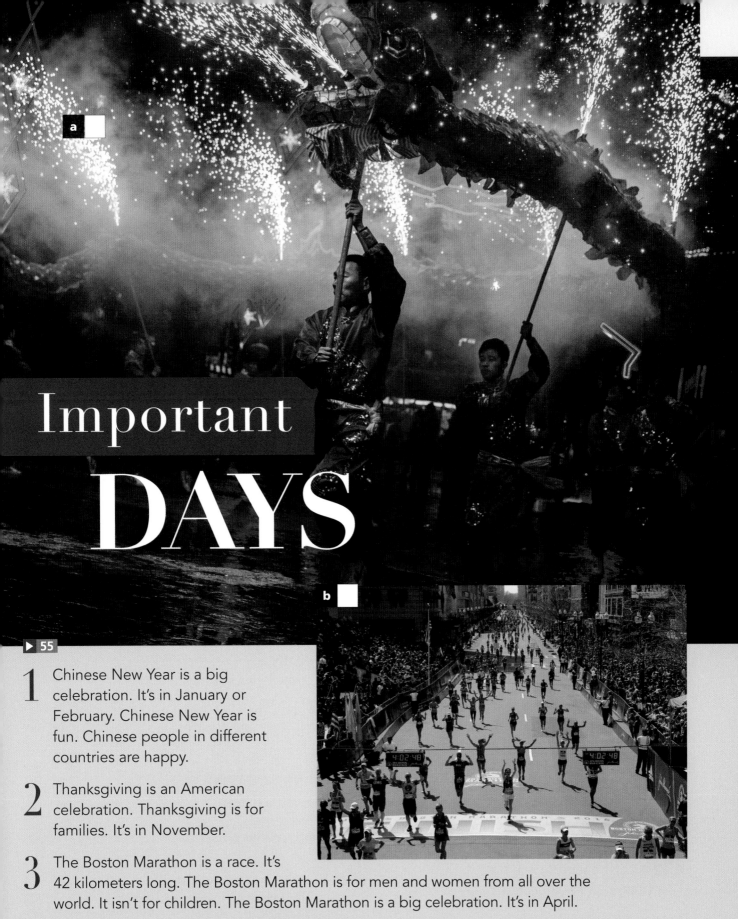

Important
DAYS

a

b

▶ 55

1 Chinese New Year is a big celebration. It's in January or February. Chinese New Year is fun. Chinese people in different countries are happy.

2 Thanksgiving is an American celebration. Thanksgiving is for families. It's in November.

3 The Boston Marathon is a race. It's 42 kilometers long. The Boston Marathon is for men and women from all over the world. It isn't for children. The Boston Marathon is a big celebration. It's in April.

4 Oscar night is a celebration of movies. It's in February. Oscar night is in Hollywood. It's for American and international movies.

3d Congratulations!

Vocabulary special occasions

1 ▶ 56 Look at the photo. Listen to the conversation. Circle the special occasion.

> a new year   a new baby   a wedding

2 ▶ 56 Put the conversation (a–e) in order (1–5). Listen and check.

a What's her name? ___
b Congratulations! _1_
c Hello, Juba. ___
d It's Juba. ___
e Thank you. We're very happy. ___

Real life special occasions

3 ▶ 57 Listen to three conversations. Match the occasions with the conversations (1–3). Then write the occasion next to each expression in the box below.

___ a wedding
___ a new year
___ a birthday

> ▶ **SPECIAL OCCASIONS**
>
> Congratulations!   _____
> Happy Birthday!   _____
> Happy New Year!   _____
> I'm very happy
> for you.   _____
> How old are you?   _____

4 Pronunciation intonation

a ▶ 58 Listen and repeat the expressions for special occasions.

b Work in pairs. Practice the conversations in track 57 of the audioscript on page 184.

Real life giving and accepting gifts

5 Work in pairs. Match the special occasions (1–3) with the gifts (a–c).

1 your friend's birthday ___
2 a new baby ___
3 your cousin's wedding ___

6 ▶ 59 Listen to the conversation. Work in pairs. Which expressions in the box below do you hear?

> ▶ **GIVING AND ACCEPTING GIFTS**
>
> **This is for** you/the baby.
> **That's** nice/very kind.
> Thanks/Thank you very much.

7 Work in pairs. Choose a special occasion. Practice the expressions for giving and accepting gifts.

> *Hi. This is for …*

3e Best wishes

Writing a greeting card

1 Writing skill contractions

a <u>Underline</u> the contractions in these sentences. Write the words in full.

1 I'm Australian. _____I am_____
2 She's French. _____
3 It isn't my birthday. _____
4 What's your name? _____
5 It's beautiful. _____
6 Who's this? _____
7 They're my cousins. _____
8 When's the party? _____

b <u>Underline</u> four contractions in these messages.

1
Hi. I'm in Spain with my brother. It's his birthday. Where are you?

2
Is it Mother's Day on Sunday?

3
Ingrid and Karl's wedding's in June. What's Karl's last name?

c Work in pairs. Rewrite these messages. Use contractions.

1
Karin's birthday is on Friday. She is twenty-one. Her party is on Saturday.

2
Hi. I am twenty-five today. Come to my party! It is at my house.

3
Hi. What is Harry's address? Is it number 5 or 7? Thanks.

2 Work in pairs. Read the cards. Answer the questions.

1 What's the occasion?
2 Who's the card from?
3 Who's the card to?

To Harry
Happy birthday!
Love and best wishes from
Katya and Bruno

thank you

To Diana
Thank you for the wedding gift. It's beautiful!
Best wishes from Ingrid and Karl

3 Write cards for a new baby and a birthday. Use some of these words.

best wishes	birthday	congratulations
from	love	on
thank you	to	your

4 Read the cards. Check the capital letters.

5 Work in pairs. Compare your cards with your partner's cards.

A dragon in a Chinese New Year celebration

Before you watch

1 Read about Chinese New Year. Complete the article with three of these words.

animals	countries	families	February

Chinese New Year
Chinese people live in ¹ _____ around the world. Chinese New Year celebrations are in January or ² _____ . Chinese people celebrate the New Year with their ³ _____ . In London, the Chinese New Year celebration is a big party.

2 Key vocabulary

a Read the sentences. Match the **bold** words (1–6) with the pictures (a–f).
1 This work is **excellent**.
2 We're at a school **reunion**.
3 The **dog** is big.
4 The **fireworks** are beautiful.
5 There are houses on the **street**.
6 I **dress up** as Spider-Man.

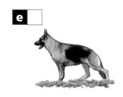

b ▶ 60 Listen and repeat the **bold** words.

While you watch

3 ◁ 3 Watch the video. Check (✓) the things you see.

☐ dragons ☐ children ☐ dogs
☐ streets ☐ food ☐ fireworks

4 ◁ 3 Watch the video again. Match the people (1–3) with their words (a–c).

1 a boy ___
2 a man ___
3 a girl ___

a It's also a family reunion.
b Lots of people dress up in red.
c Absolutely excellent.

5 ◁ 3 Complete the sentences. Watch the video and check.

1 It's Chinese New Year. This celebration is in _____ .
2 It's traditional to give _____ .
3 In the _____ , people watch fireworks.

After you watch

6 Work in pairs. Test your memory. Write six things from the video. Compare with your partner.

> *There are fireworks in the street.*

7 Work in pairs. Translate the sentences from the video into your own language. Compare with your partner.

1 It's really great.
2 Red is the lucky color for Chinese.

UNIT 3 REVIEW AND MEMORY BOOSTER

Grammar

1 Complete the sentences with these words.

her	his	our	their

1 This card is for Ellie and Greg. What's _____ address?
2 A: Is that David's sister?
  B: No, it's _____ friend.
3 This is my wife and these are _____ three children.
4 A: Your baby is beautiful! What's _____ name?
  B: It's Elena.

2 Complete the sentences with the possessive form.

1 This is _____ .
  (Jin / family)
2 This is _____ .
  (Sandra / car)
3 They're _____ .
  (Toni / keys)
4 This is _____ .
  (Diana / phone)

3 ›› MB Work in pairs. Talk about things in class.

> This is Emily's book.   This is Alan's pen.

I CAN
talk about people and possessions (possessive adjectives and possessive 's)

Vocabulary

4 Match the words for men and women.

1 brother ○   ○ daughter
2 father ○   ○ grandmother
3 grandfather ○   ○ mother
4 husband ○   ○ sister
5 son ○   ○ wife

5 ›› MB Work in pairs. Ask and answer questions about family. Take turns.

> What's your ...'s name?

6 Circle the correct option.

1 My sister is tall and I'm *short / old*.
2 What color are the baby's *eyes / hair*?
3 My son is *tall / young* —five years old.

7 ›› MB Work in pairs. Take turns.
Student A: Say a month.
Student B: Say the next month.

I CAN
talk about my family and friends
talk about months and ages

Real life

8 Work in pairs. Put the words in order. Then match 1–3 with a–c.

1 you / gift / a / here's / for / . ___
2 is / how old / he / today / ? ___
3 very / kind / is / that / . ___

a is / eighteen / he / .
b much / thank / very / you / .
c are / welcome / you / .

9 Work in pairs. Practice the exchanges in Exercise 8. Use contractions.

I CAN
talk about special occasions
give and accept gifts

Unit 4 Cities

Evening in the city of Astana, Kazakhstan

FEATURES

1 Look at the photo. Find these things.

| buildings | a tower | a garden | trees |

2 Read the photo caption. Circle the name of the city and the country.

3 ▶ 61 Listen. Are the sentences true (T) or false (F)?

1 Astana is the capital city of Kazakhstan. T F
2 The buildings in Astana are tall. T F
3 Astana is a dirty city. T F

4 Work in pairs. Talk about your town or city.

I'm from Brasília. It's in Brazil. It's modern.

Is it the capital?

Yes, it is.

4a In the city

Vocabulary places in a town

1 ▶ 62 Listen and match the photos (1–10) with the words (a–j).

a a bank
b a museum
c a bus station
d a cafe
e a parking lot
f an information center
g a movie theater
h a market
i a train station
j a park

2 ▶ 62 Listen again and repeat the places.

3 Work in pairs. Are the places in Exercise 1 in your town or city? What are their names?

> *The movie theater in my town is called the Phoenix.*

Reading

4 Work in pairs. Look at the map. Find four places on Pine Street.

5 Read the four comments. Write the places. Are the comments good (G) or bad (B)?

1 The _____ is new.   G   B
2 The _____ is popular.   G   B
3 The _____ is old.   G   B
4 The _____ is on   G   B
   Bush Street.

a bank
b Transport Museum
c bus station
d Pine Cafe
e parking lot
f Tourist Information Center
g Roxy Movie Theater
h Central Market
i train station
j Green Park

The museum isn't very good. It's old. It's near the railway station.
Berta

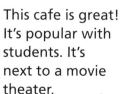

This cafe is great! It's popular with students. It's next to a movie theater.
Artem

Grammar prepositions of place

▶ PREPOSITIONS OF PLACE

●	●●	● ∣ ●	● ●
on	next to	opposite	near

Now look at page 164.

6 Look at the grammar box. <u>Underline</u> the prepositions in the four comment boxes.

7 Read the sentences. Look at the map. Are the sentences true (T) or false (F)?

1 The museum is on   T   F
   Pine Street.
2 The cafe is next to the   T   F
   movie theater.
3 The market is opposite   T   F
   the movie theater.

8 Look at the map. Circle the correct option.

1 The bank is *next to / opposite* the market.
2 The movie theater is *on / near* Pine Street.
3 The parking lot is *near / next to* the museum.

4 The information center is *next to / opposite* the bus station.
5 The bus station is *on / next to* the park.

9 ▶ 63 Listen to four conversations about places on the map. Write the number of the conversation (1–4) next to the places.

___ bank   ___ information center
___ parking lot   ___ train station

10 ▶ 63 Listen again. Work in pairs. Look at the map. Is the information correct?

Speaking myLife

11 Work in pairs. Practice the conversations in track 63 of the audioscript on page 184.

12 Work in pairs. Ask and answer questions about places on the map.

   Excuse me?
           Yes?

   Where's the market?

13 Work in pairs. Ask and answer questions about four places in your town.

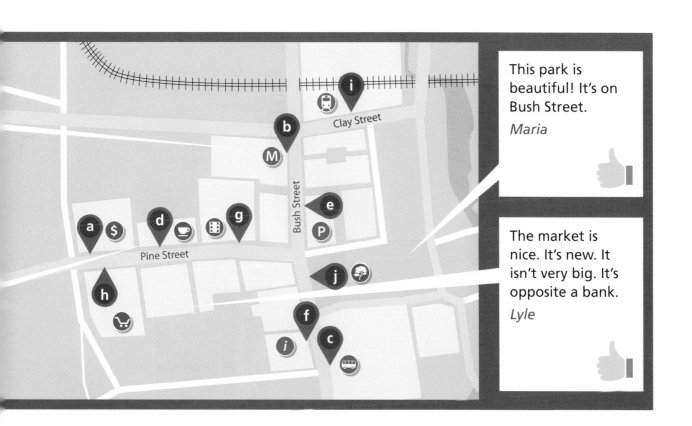

This park is beautiful! It's on Bush Street.
Maria

The market is nice. It's new. It isn't very big. It's opposite a bank.
Lyle

4b Tourist information

Listening

1 ▶ 64 Listen to two conversations. Number the sentences in order.

1 ___ Good morning.
___ Is this a map of New York?
_1_ Hi.
___ It's near Fifth Avenue ... here it is.
___ No. **That**'s the wrong map. **This** is a map of New York.
___ Oh, OK. Where's the Guggenheim Museum?

2 ___ And bus schedules?
___ Good afternoon. Where are the schedules, please?
___ OK, thanks.
___ **Those** are bus schedules, next to the door.
___ Well, **these** are train schedules, here.

2 Work in pairs. Practice the conversations in Exercise 1.

Grammar *this, that, these, those*

▶ **THIS, THAT, THESE, THOSE**

Is **this** a map of the city?

That's a map of the city.

Are **these** maps of the city?

Those are maps of the city.

Now look at page 164.

3 Look at the grammar box. Write S (singular) or P (plural).
1 this, that _____ 2 these, those _____

4 ▶ 65 Read the conversations. Write *this, that, these,* and *those*. Listen and check.

1
Is _____ a train schedule?

No, it's a bus schedule.

2
Excuse me. Are _____ pens or pencils?

They're pencils. The pens are next to the maps.

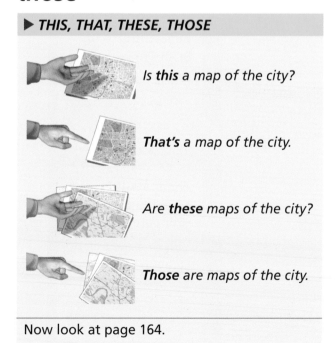

3
Excuse me. Are _____ maps of Astana?

Yes, they are.

4
Is _____ guidebook in English?

Which guidebook?

The book next to you.

No, it isn't. It's in Spanish.

The Skytree

▶ 67

What is it?
It's a tower.

Where is it?
It's in Tokyo, Japan.
It's near Asakusa
Station.

When is it open?
It's open every day.

Why is it famous?
It's new. It's a
symbol of Tokyo.

The Eiffel Tower

What is it?
It's a tower.

Where is it?
It's in Paris, France.
It's next to the
Seine river.

When is it open?
It's open every day.

Why is it famous?
It's old. It's a symbol
of France.

5 Pronunciation *th* /ð/

a ▶ 66 Listen and repeat the conversations from Exercise 4.

b Practice the *th* sound in these words.

> this   that   these   those   there   they   the

Reading

6 Read about *The Skytree* and *The Eiffel Tower*. Circle the correct option.

1 The *Skytree* / *Eiffel Tower* is in Europe.
2 The *Skytree* / *Eiffel Tower* is new.
3 The *Skytree* / *Eiffel Tower* is near a river.

Grammar question words

▶ **QUESTION WORDS**

What is it?	***When*** is it open?
Where is it?	***Why*** is it famous?

Now look at page 164.

7 Complete the questions with the correct question word.

1 Q: _____ are you?
   A: I'm in the park.
2 Q: _____ is the museum open?
   A: Every day.
3 Q: _____ is the name of this street?
   A: Pine Street.
4 Q: _____ is this place famous?
   A: It's very old.
5 Q: _____ is this?
   A: It's in Italy.
6 Q: _____ is your vacation?
   A: It's in June.

Speaking *my*Life

8 Work in pairs. Ask and answer questions about two places.
Student A: Turn to page 153.
Student B: Turn to page 155.

4c Time zones

Vocabulary the time

1 ▶ 68 Match the times with the clocks. Listen, check, and repeat.

1 `11:00 AM` ○ ○ eight twenty ___

2 `09:30 AM` ○ ○ eleven o'clock ___

3 `08:20 PM` ○ ○ three fifty-five ___

4 `03:55 PM` ○ ○ nine thirty ___

2 Write M (morning), A (afternoon), or E (evening) for the times in Exercise 1.

3 Work in pairs. Ask and answer questions.

What time is	your the	English class? school open? lunch?

Critical thinking thinking about your country

4 What time do people do each activity in your country? Write M (morning), A (afternoon), or E (evening).

Children go to school ___

People are at work ___

People are in bed ___

Children go home ___

People have dinner ___

Reading

5 Read *Time zones.* It's noon in London. Write the names of two cities.

London: 12 p.m.
1 _____ : 4 a.m.
2 _____ : 8 p.m.

6 Work in pairs. Look at the map. It's noon in London. What time is it in these places?
1 New York   _____
2 Rio de Janeiro   _____
3 Johannesburg   _____
4 Jakarta   _____
5 Sydney   _____

7 What time and day is it where you are now? What time and day is it in New York now?

8 Word focus *at*

a Underline three sentences with *at* in *Time zones* on page 51.

b ▶ 69 Complete the conversations with these expressions. Listen and check.

at five o'clock   at home   at school   at work

1 A: Where are your children? Are they here?
   B: No. It's 10 a.m. They're _____ .

2 A: Sandy, what time is your train?
   B: It's _____ .

3 A: Hi, Tom. Are you _____ ?
   B: No, I'm not. It's a holiday today. I'm _____ .

Speaking *my* **Life**

9 Work in pairs. Ask about different days and times. Take turns.

at home	at school	in a cafe
in bed	in the city	in the classroom

It's Tuesday. It's nine thirty in the evening. Where are you?

I'm at home.

TIME ZONES

In London, it's twelve noon. Shops and offices are open. People are at work. Children are at school. In Perth, Australia, it's eight o'clock in the evening. Schools are closed and children are at home. People are in cafes and restaurants. In Los Angeles, it's four o'clock in the morning. People aren't at work. They're at home. They're in bed.

There are many different time zones in the world. Lima and New York are in the same time zone. Singapore and Perth are in the same time zone. Perth and Sydney are in different time zones. The International Date Line is the end of one day and the beginning of the next day. It's only 80 kilometers from Russia to Alaska, but Sunday in Russia is Saturday in Alaska.

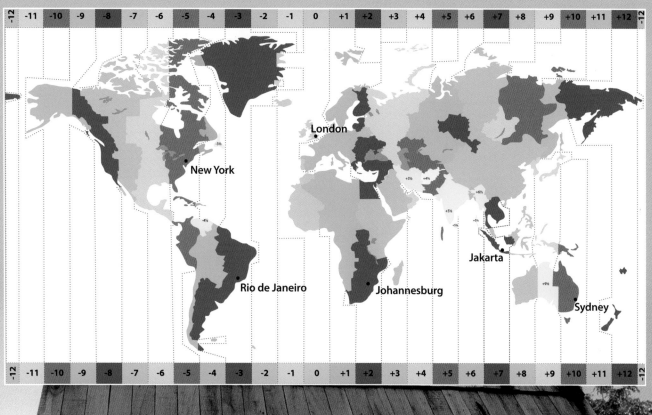

Taveuni Island, Fiji

4d Two teas, please

Vocabulary snacks

1 ▶71 Look at the photos (a–h). Match the words (1–8) with the photos. Listen, check, and repeat.

1	apple	5	salad
2	banana	6	sandwich
3	coffee	7	tea
4	fruit juice	8	water

a  **b**

c **d**

e **f**

g

h

Real life buying snacks

2 ▶72 Listen to three conversations. Complete the conversations with expressions for buying snacks.

1 A: Hi. Can I help you?
   C: ¹ _____
   A: ² _____
   C: Small.
   A: Anything else?
   C: ³ _____

2 A: Hi. Can I help you?
   C: ⁴ _____
   A: Anything else?
   C: Yes. A salad.
   A: OK. ⁵ _____

3 A: ⁶ _____
   C: A tea and a fruit juice, please.
   A: ⁷ _____
   C: Yes. Two sandwiches, please.
   A: OK. Here you are. Eleven dollars, please.

> ▶ **BUYING SNACKS**
>
> | | |
> |---|---|
> | Can I help you? | Anything else? |
> | Two coffees, please. | No, thanks. |
> | Can I have a bottle of water, please? | Four dollars, please. |
> | | Here you are. |
> | Large or small? | |

3 Pronunciation linking with *can*

a ▶73 Listen and repeat these sentences.

1 Can‿I help you?
2 Can‿I have a bottle of water, please?

b Work in pairs. Practice the conversations in Exercise 2.

4 Work in pairs. Buy snacks from your partner.

Hi. Can I help you?

Two teas, please.

4e See you soon

Writing a text message

1 Read the text message. Answer the
questions.

1 Who is the message to? _____
2 Who is it from? _____
3 Where is she? _____

Chats (2)   **Jen**
             available

Hi Sandra. We're in Bangkok. It's great!
Our hotel is big and new. It's near the
market in our photo. The markets are
famous here. Thai people are friendly
and Thai food is great.

11.55

2 Read the text message again. Underline:

1 one adjective to describe Bangkok
2 two adjectives to describe the hotel
3 one adjective to describe the markets
4 one adjective to describe the people
5 one adjective to describe the food

3 Writing skill *and*

a Read the text message again. Circle *and* in
two sentences.

b Work in pairs. Read the pairs of sentences.
Write one new sentence.

1 The hotel is big. The hotel is new.
   *The hotel is big **and** new.*
2 The park is open on Saturdays. The
   park is open on Sundays.
3 The town is old. The town is beautiful.
4 It's famous in America. It's famous in
   Europe.

c Work in pairs. Read the pairs of sentences.
Write one new sentence.

1 Thai people are friendly. Thai food
   is great.
   *Thai people are friendly **and** Thai food
   is great.*
2 Our hotel is modern. The room is clean.
3 The streets are clean. The houses are
   beautiful.
4 The airport is small. The plane is old.
5 The park is next to our hotel. The
   market is near.

4 Choose a place you know. Write a text
message to your partner. Write about
three of these things. Use *and*.

- the town / city   • the food
- the hotel   • the people

5 Check your text message. Check the
adjectives and your spelling.

6 Exchange text messages with your
partner. Where is your partner?

4f Where's that?

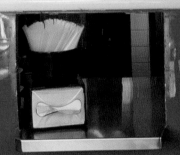

A snack bar near the beach

Before you watch

1 Look at the photo and the caption on page 54. Where is this place?

_____

2 Key vocabulary

a Read the sentences (1–3). Match the **bold** words with the pictures (a–c).

1 Fifth Avenue is a big **shopping street** in New York City.
2 The name of the cafe is on the **sign**.
3 The George Washington **Bridge** is in New York City. It's on the Hudson River.

b ▶ 74 Listen and repeat the **bold** words.

3 Work in pairs. Say where these things are in your city or town.

- ☐ a bank
- ☐ a bridge
- ☐ a bus station
- ☐ a cafe
- ☐ a garden
- ☐ a market
- ☐ a movie theater
- ☐ a museum
- ☐ a park
- ☐ a parking lot
- ☐ a shopping street
- ☐ a snack bar
- ☐ a train station
- ☐ an information center

While you watch

4 ◼4 Watch the video. Check (✓) the things in Exercise 3 that you see in the video.

5 ◼4 Watch the video. Where are the cities? Match the city (1–3) with the continent.

North America ____
Asia ____
Europe ____

6 Work in pairs. What are the names of the three cities? Do you agree with your partner?

1 a Madrid b San Francisco c Tokyo
2 a Madrid b Hong Kong c Washington
3 a Beijing b San Francisco c Rome

After you watch

7 Look at the questions and answers from the video. Complete the questions.

A: That's beautiful. [1] _____'s that?
B: It's in the city. It's a park with a lake.
A: [2] _____'s that? Is that you next to the lake?
B: No, it isn't.

A: [3] _____'s that? A park?
B: It's a garden—and a nice cafe next to the garden.

8 Match the places with each city from the video (1–3). Then write sentences about one of the cities.

Atocha Station ____
Fisherman's Wharf ____
Shinjuku district ____
the Golden Gate Bridge ____
the Imperial Palace ____
the Prado Museum ____

UNIT 4 REVIEW AND MEMORY BOOSTER

Grammar

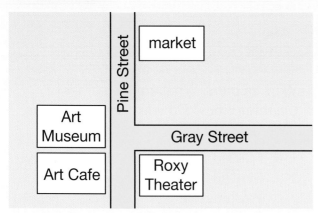

1 Look at the map. Complete the paragraph with the words below.

next to	near	on	opposite

The Art Cafe is a new cafe. It's ¹ _____ Pine Street. It's ² _____ the Art Museum. It's open from 10 a.m. to 6 p.m. from Mondays to Saturdays. It's ³ _____ the Roxy Theater and it's ⁴ _____ Pine Street market.

2 Complete the questions about the Art Cafe.

1 _____ is the cafe?
2 _____ is it open? 9 a.m.?
3 _____ is next to the Art Cafe?

3 ≫ MB Work in pairs. Ask and answer the questions from Exercise 2.

4 Circle the correct option.

1 Is *these* / *this* the bus to Boston?
2 Are *that* / *those* apples?

I CAN	
describe the location of places (prepositions of place)	☐
ask and answer questions (question words)	☐
use *this*, *that*, *these*, and *those* correctly	☐

Vocabulary

5 Complete the words for places in a town.

1 b _ n k
2 _ n f _ r m _ t _ _ n c _ nte _
3 tr _ _ n st _ t _ _ n

6 ≫ MB Work in pairs. Where are the places in Exercise 5 in your town?

7 ≫ MB Work in pairs. Take turns.
Student A: Choose a clock. Say the time.
Student B: Point to the clock.

8 Complete the menu with these words.

salad	fruit juice	coffee	sandwiches

The Art Cafe

Hot drinks
tea	$1.00
¹ _____	$1.50

Cold drinks
water	$1.00
² _____	$1.50

Snacks
³ _____	$2.00
⁴ _____	$2.00
cake	$1.50

I CAN	
talk about places in a town	☐
say the time	☐
talk about snacks	☐

Real life

9 Put the conversation in order (1–8).

____ Large or small?
____ Can I have two teas, please?
____ OK. Six dollars, please.
____ No, thanks.
____ Hello. Can I help you?
____ Anything else?
____ Small, please.
____ Here you are.

10 Practice the conversation in Exercise 9.

I CAN	
buy snacks	☐

Unit 5 My things

The "jetman" in the air

FEATURES

1 Look at the photo and the caption. Where is the "jetman"? _____

2 ▶ 75 Read the sentences. Then listen. Are the sentences true (T) or false (F)?

1 Yves Rossy is from Switzerland.   T   F
2 He can fly.   T   F
3 He's in the air for nine minutes.   T   F

3 ▶ 75 Listen again. Work in pairs. Why is the photo fantastic?

4 Work in pairs. <u>Underline</u> two things that can fly.

| birds | dogs | lions | planes |

5a Robots and people

ROBOTS AND PEOPLE

▶ 76

The woman on the left is 69-year-old Akiko Nabeshima. She's in a supermarket in Japan. She's with a robot. The robot is from Keihanna Science City near Kyoto. This robot can see and it can speak. It can move, but it can't run. It can carry things—for example, Akiko's basket. Robots are amazing. They can help people in their lives.

Reading

1 Work in pairs. Look at the photo. Find:

| two women | a robot | a child | a basket |

2 Read *Robots and people*. <u>Underline</u>:
 1 four things this robot can do.
 2 one thing this robot can't do.

Grammar *can/can't*

▶ *CAN/CAN'T*

| *I/You*
He/She/It
We/You/They | **can**
can't | *see.*
run. |

(can't = cannot)

Now look at page 166.

3 Circle the correct option to make a true sentence.

Robots *can / can't* help people.

4 Work in pairs. Write sentences with *can* and *can't*.

 1 robots / move ✓
   Robots can move.
 2 robots / speak ✓
 3 robots / carry things ✓
 4 people / fly ✗
 5 I / speak English ✓

5 Pronunciation *can/can't*

▶ 77 Listen and check your sentences from Exercise 4. Listen again and repeat.

Vocabulary abilities

6 ▶ 78 Listen. Check (✓) the sentences that are true for you.

☐ I can cook.

☐ I can speak English.

☐ I can play ping-pong.

☐ I can drive a car.

☐ I can ride a bike.

☐ I can swim.

☐ I can sing.

☐ I can play the piano.

7 Work in pairs. Read the sentences in Exercise 6 to your partner. Use *can't* for sentences that aren't true for you.

> *I can ride a bike.*　　*I can't drive a car.*

Listening

8 ▶ 79 Listen to an interview about a robot. Are the sentences true (T) or false (F)?
1 Tomo is an American robot.　　T　F
2 Tomo is a new kind of robot.　　T　F
3 "Tomo" means "friend."　　T　F

9 ▶ 79 Listen again. What are the answers to the questions? Write ✓ (can) or ✗ (can't).

1 Can Tomo speak Japanese?　　___
2 Can she play the piano?　　___
3 Can she swim?　　___

Grammar *can* questions and short answers

▶ **CAN QUESTIONS and SHORT ANSWERS**

Can	I/you he/she/it we/you/they	speak Japanese? swim?
Yes, No,	I/you he/she/it we/you/they	can. can't.

Now look at page 166.

10 Work in pairs. Look at the grammar box. Write short answers to the questions in Exercise 9.

Speaking myLife

11 Work in pairs. Ask and answer questions about the abilities in Exercise 6.

> *Can you cook?*　　*Yes, I can. / No, I can't.*

5b Our things

Vocabulary possessions

1 Look at the pictures. Match the words (1–8) with the pictures (a–h).

1 a camera
2 a cat
3 glasses
4 a guitar
5 a motorcycle
6 photos
7 a soccer ball
8 a watch

2 ▶ 80 Listen and check your answers from Exercise 1. Repeat the words.

3 Work in pairs. Test your partner. Take turns.
Student A: Point to an object.
Student B: Name the object.

Listening

4 ▶ 81 Listen to four people. Write their possessions.

person 1 _____

person 2 _____

person 3 _____

person 4 _____

5 ▶ 81 Listen again. Complete the descriptions.

1 It has a _____ on it—1921. It's very _____ .

2 He has _____ colored eyes. One is _____ and one is _____ .

3 Astronauts and _____ wear the same watch. It's very _____ .

4 It's from the _____ World Cup. It's from a game between Portugal and _____ .

6 Work in pairs. Why are the possessions interesting?

Grammar *have/has*

▶ **HAVE/HAS**		
I/You/We/You/They	**have**	*a motorcycle.*
He/She/It	**has**	*glasses.*

Now look at page 166.

7 Look at the grammar box. Look at the sentences. Circle the correct option.

1 My baseball *have / has* a signature on it.
2 My friends *have / has* a piano.

8 Complete the sentences with *has* or *have*.

1 I _____ a bicycle. It's new.
2 My brother _____ two cameras. They're expensive.
3 My sister _____ a bag. It's black.
4 My friends _____ a car. It's small.
5 I _____ two sisters. They _____ brown eyes.

9 Pronunciation *have/has*

a ▶ 82 Listen and check your sentences from Exercise 8. Listen again and repeat.

b Work in pairs. Tell your partner about two of your possessions.

> *I have a camera. It isn't new. It's a Nikon.*

Grammar *be* + adjective

▶ **BE + ADJECTIVE**
*My cat is **beautiful**.*
*Your children are **young**.*
*His camera isn't **expensive**.*
*Are these glasses **new**?*

Now look at page 166.

10 Look at the grammar box. Are adjectives the same with singular and plural nouns? Or are they different? _____

11 Write the words in order.

1 car / our / new / isn't

_____

2 old / is / camera / your / ?

_____

3 beautiful / children / our / are

_____

4 interesting / are / her / photos / very

_____

5 bag / black and white / his / is / ?

_____

Speaking *myLife*

12 Work in pairs. Talk about three of your possessions, animals, or family members.

5c Technology and me

Vocabulary technology

1 Look at the objects. Number the words (1–6).

a battery	____	a webcam	____
a camera	____	an app	____
a screen	____	headphones	____

a laptop **1**

a tablet **2**

3

4

a cell phone **5**

6

2 Work in pairs. What do you use for each: a cell phone or a laptop?

1 talk to people
2 take photos
3 play music
4 send emails

Reading

3 Read the *Intelligent travel blog*. Work in pairs. Underline these adjectives. What do they describe?

new	expensive	good
old	nice	great

Critical thinking who said it?

4 In the *Intelligent travel blog:*

1 Who asks the questions? _____
2 Who answers the questions?_____

Grammar adjective + noun

> ▶ **ADJECTIVE + NOUN**
>
> 1a This **camera** is **old**.
> 1b It's an **old camera**.
> 2a These **headphones** are **great**.
> 2b They're **great headphones**.

Now look at page 166.

5 Look at the words in **bold** in the grammar box. Circle the adjectives and underline the nouns.

6 Look at sentences 1b and 2b in the grammar box. Is the adjective before or after the noun? _____

7 Work in pairs. Read the pairs of sentences. Write one new sentence. Put the adjective before the noun.

1 I have a bag. It's nice.
  I have a nice bag.
2 That's a laptop. It's fantastic.
3 Jack has a passport. It's new.
4 I have two TVs. They're black.
5 We have a map of the world. It's old.

Speaking my Life

8 Work in pairs. Talk about your favorite piece of technology.

What's your favorite piece of technology?

My tablet.

INTELLIGENT TRAVEL

▶ 83

This week, we ask a travel writer about the technology in her travel bag. Here are her answers.

Tell us about your travel bag.

My travel bag is my "mobile office." There are many things in my bag. I have them with me on every trip. It isn't a small bag!

Which things are expensive?

Well, I have a new camera. It can take hundreds of photos. And my laptop is expensive, too. It has a good battery—I can work on planes and trains with no problems.

What about your phone?

I have an old phone. It has a nice camera. I can talk to my family at home, and they can see me.

What about music?

My phone has an app for music, and I have great headphones. I can listen to music all the time.

5d How much is it?

Vocabulary money and prices

1 Work in pairs. Match these countries with their money. Write $ (dollars), € (euros), or £ (pounds).

Australia ___ Belgium ___
Germany ___ the US ___
the UK ___ Canada ___

2 ▶ 84 Listen and repeat the prices.

a $2.30 d €3.75
b €13.50 e $17.80
c €15.00 f $18.00

3 Pronunciation numbers

a ▶ 85 Listen and circle the correct price.

1 $13.00 $30.00 4 $16.00 $60.00
2 $14.00 $40.00 5 $17.00 $70.00
3 $15.00 $50.00 6 $18.00 $80.00

b ▶ 85 Listen again and repeat the prices.

Real life shopping

4 ▶ 86 Listen to three conversations. Match the conversations (1–3) with the products. There is one extra product.

5 ▶ 86 Listen to the conversations again. Circle the correct price.

1 $15 $30 $80
2 $19.50 $65.60 $95.50
3 $5.99 $9.99 $99

6 Look at the expressions for shopping. Who says each expression? Write C (customer) or S (store clerk).

> **▶ SHOPPING**
>
> ___ Excuse me.
> ___ Can I help you?
> ___ I'd like these sunglasses, please.
> ___ How much is this alarm clock?
> ___ How much are these memory sticks?
> ___ It's/They're $30.
> ___ That's $19.50, please.
> ___ Can I pay with dollars/cash/a credit card?

7 Work in pairs. Look at track 86 of the audioscript on page 185. Practice the conversations.

8 Work in pairs. Take turns to buy a product.
Store clerk: Decide the price.
Customer: Decide how much you can pay.

an alarm clock ___

books ___

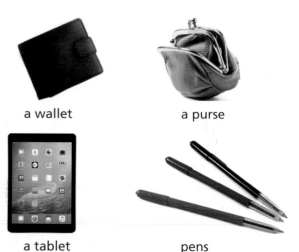

a wallet   a purse

a tablet   pens

sunglasses ___

memory sticks ___

5e Can you help me?

Writing an email

1 Read the first email below.

1 Who is the email from? _____
2 Who is the email to? _____

2 Read the reply. Complete the chart.

	Positive +	Negative -
Tablets	can write on the screen	
Laptops	have a touchscreen have a keyboard fast	

Computer Life *Weekly*

Email mike@computerlifeweekly.com

Hi Mike,

I'm a student at college. I'd like a new computer. My PC is old and slow. I can buy a laptop or a tablet. I can't decide. Can you help me?

Eliza

Hi Eliza,

Tablets have good screens, but they're small. You can write on the screen. That's great. Laptops can have a touchscreen or a keyboard. Good laptops are fast, but they're expensive. I hope this helps.

Mike
Computer Life

screen

keyboard

3 Writing skill *but*

a <u>Underline</u> two sentences with *but* in Mike's reply.

b Work in pairs. Read the pairs of sentences. Write one new sentence with *but*. Add a comma (,) before *but*.

1 This tablet is great. It's expensive.
2 The screen isn't big. It's nice.
3 My car is old. It's fast.
4 My PC isn't old. It's slow.
5 The dog is small. It's loud.
6 The book is old. It's interesting.

c Complete the sentences with *and* or *but*.

1 The wallets are very expensive, _____ they're nice.
2 My laptop is big, _____ it's heavy.
3 Your car is small, _____ it's fast.
4 These cameras are old, _____ they're good.
5 Learning English is easy, _____ it's interesting.

4 Complete the email with these words. One word is extra.

bus	bicycle	can	can't
cheap	fast	motorcycle	slow

I'm a student at college. The [1] _____ to college is [2] _____ , but it's [3] _____—more than one hour. I can buy a [4] _____ or a [5] _____ . I [6] _____ decide. [7] _____ you help me?

5 Work in pairs. Reply to the email in Exercise 4. Say one positive and one negative thing about bicycles and motorcycles.

5f What's your favorite gadget?

People use their phones at a concert.

Before you watch

1 Look at the photo on page 66. What gadgets can you see? _____

2 Key vocabulary

a Read the sentences. Match the **bold** words (1–4) with the pictures (a–d).

1 My **kitchen** is very small. I can cook in it, but I can't eat in it.
2 I can make great coffee with my new **coffee machine.**
3 I can cook lots of different food in my **microwave oven.**
4 My **office** is in the center of town.

b ▶ 87 Listen and repeat the **bold** words.

3 Work in pairs. Tell your partner what gadgets you have and where they are.

a camera	a memory stick
a coffee machine	a microwave oven
a laptop	a cell phone

I have a laptop in my office.

While you watch

4 ◻5 Watch the video. Work in pairs. What are Ashley and Clare's favorite gadgets?

5 Work in pairs. What can you remember about the two gadgets?

6 ◻5 Watch the video again. Circle the options (a–c) you hear.

Ashley's favorite gadget:
a has a diary.   c has a camera.
b is expensive.

Clare's favorite gadget:
a is basic.   c can make coffee
b is Italian.   in two minutes.

7 ◻5 Can you remember who says these things? Write A (Ashley) or C (Clare). Then watch the video again and check.

1 _____ is very busy.
2 _____ has a new gadget.
3 _____ can talk to the gadget.

After you watch

8 Complete the sentences with the words.

camera	email	friends	office
phone	photos	photos	

And this phone has a great [1] _____ . I can take fantastic [2] _____ and I can send them to my [3] _____ or to the computer in my [4] _____ . The [5] _____ from this phone are really, really good! And I can talk to my [6] _____ ! I can say, "Send this photo to John." Or, "Send an [7] _____ to my office." Or, "Call home."

basic	coffee	expensive	friends
kitchen	microwave	ten	

Some coffee machines are [8] _____ , but my new machine is a [9] _____ machine and it isn't expensive. It's in my [10] _____ next to my [11] _____ .
I have a lot of gadgets in my kitchen. I can make a cup of [12] _____ in two minutes. And it's fantastic coffee. I have [13] _____ different types of coffee! So I can make different types of coffee for my [14] _____ .

9 What's your favorite gadget? Why?

UNIT 5 REVIEW AND MEMORY BOOSTER

Grammar

1 Work in pairs. Ask and answer questions about Lynn. Use *can*. Take turns.

drive a car ✓	speak Spanish ✗
ride a bicycle ✗	speak Japanese ✓
play the piano ✓	write in French ✗

2 ▶▶ MB Work in pairs. Make true sentences about yourself with the abilities in Exercise 1.

3 Complete the sentences with *have* or *has*.

1 I _____ brown eyes.
2 My brother _____ red hair.
3 My husband and I _____ a car.
4 Our friends _____ a nice house.
5 My friend _____ glasses.
6 My dad _____ a new camera.

4 ▶▶ MB Work in pairs. Make true or false sentences with *I have* + noun and these adjectives. Say *true* or *false* to your partner.

beautiful	expensive	fantastic	great
interesting	new	nice	old

I have a new car.
        False.

I CAN	
talk about abilities (*can*)	
talk about possessions and features (*have*)	
describe objects (adjective + noun)	

Vocabulary

5 Circle the correct object (a–c).

1 You can take photos with a _____ .
  a camera   b cat   c motorcycle
2 You can play music with a _____ .
  a soccer ball b guitar c photo
3 You can listen to music with _____ .
  a batteries b headphones c a screen

6 ▶▶ MB Work in pairs. Take turns.
Student A: Choose a tag. Say the price.
Student B: Point to the price tag.

$14.99   **$50** $71.40 $13.30

I CAN	
talk about possessions	
talk about technology	
talk about money	

Real life

7 Complete the conversation between a customer (C) and a store clerk (S) with these words. One word is extra.

are	help	here	like
much	pay	that's	they're

S: Can I ¹_____ you?
C: Yes. How ²_____ are these glasses?
S: ³_____ $65. And those ones are $89.
C: OK. I'd ⁴_____ these ones, please.
S: ⁵_____ you are. ⁶_____ $65.
C: Can I ⁷_____ with a credit card?
S: Yes, of course.

8 Work in pairs. Practice the conversation in Exercise 7. Change the object and the price.

I CAN	
buy things	

Unit 6 We love it!

Soccer fans in
Soweto, South Africa

FEATURES

1 Look at the photo. What's the sport? _____

2 ▶ 88 Look at these numbers. Say the numbers. Listen
and circle the correct option in sentences 1 and 2.

100 = one hundred	1,000,000 = one million
1,000 = one thousand	

1 About 270 *thousand / million* people play soccer.
2 Soccer is popular in about two *hundred / thousand*
countries.

3 Work in pairs. Take turns to say the numbers.

13,000,000	300	20,000	70,000,000

4 Work in groups. Answer the questions.

1 Which sports are popular in your country?
2 What sports can you play?

6a My sport

Vocabulary sports

1 Work in pairs. Match the words (1–5) with the photos (a–e).

1 basketball   4 running
2 cycling   5 tennis
3 swimming

2 ▶ 89 Write the words from Exercise 1. Listen and check.

1 _Running_ is a sport in the Olympics.
2 _____ is a sport in water.
3 _____ is a sport with bicycles.
4 _____ is a sport with a ball for two or four people.
5 _____ is a sport with a ball for two teams.

Reading

MY SPORT

▶ 90

Hi! My name's Laura. My sport is the triathlon—swimming, cycling, and running. It's swimming for about one kilometer, cycling for forty kilometers, and running for ten kilometers. I like swimming and cycling, but I don't like running. My best time is three hours and five minutes. It's not bad, but it's not very good. The best Olympic time for women is one hour and fifty-six minutes.

3 Look at the photo. What's the sport?

_____

4 Work in pairs. Read about Laura. Answer the questions.

1 What are the three parts of the triathlon?
2 How long is each part of the triathlon?

Grammar *like*

▶ LIKE

I/You/We/You/They	like don't like	basketball. tennis.
(don't = do not)		

Now look at page 168.

5 Look at the grammar box. Read about Laura again and <u>underline</u> the sentence with *like* and *don't like*.

6 Work in pairs. Write sentences with *like* (☺) or *don't like* (☹).

1 I / tennis. ☺
   I like tennis.
2 I / swimming. ☺
3 I / soccer. ☹
4 My friends / sports. ☺
5 I / basketball. ☹

7 ▶ 91 Listen and check your sentences from Exercise 6. Listen again and repeat.

8 Work in pairs. Change the sentences in Exercise 6 so that they are true for you. Say the sentences to your partner.

I don't like tennis.

Listening

9 ▶ 92 Listen to a conversation about sports. Check (✓) the questions you hear.

☐ Do you like sports?
☐ Do your friends like sports?
☐ What sports do you like?

10 ▶ 92 Listen to the conversation again. Circle the answers to the questions.

1 Q: Do you like sports?
   A: *I love sports! / No, I don't.*
2 Q: What sports do you like?
   A: My favorite sports are *running and swimming / tennis and soccer.*

Grammar *like* questions and short answers

▶ LIKE QUESTIONS and SHORT ANSWERS

Do	I/you/we/you/they	like	tennis?
Yes, No,	I/you/we/you/they	do. don't.	

Now look at page 168.

11 Look at the grammar box. What's the question form of *like*? _____

12 Look at the grammar box again. Complete these questions and short answers.

1 _____ you _____ swimming?
   Yes, _____ _____ .
2 _____ they _____ cycling?
   No, _____ _____ .

13 ▶ 93 Work in pairs. Write questions with *like*. Listen to two conversations and check. What are the answers?

1 people in your family / sports?
2 what sports / you / on TV?
3 you / basketball?
4 you / swimming or cycling?

14 Pronunciation *do you …?*

a ▶ 94 Listen and repeat the questions.

b Work in pairs. Ask and answer the questions in Exercise 13.

Speaking myLife

15 Work as a class. Write three sports you like. Ask your classmates *Do you like* questions about these sports, and write the names of the people who like the same sports as you.

Bruno, do you like tennis?

Yes, I do. I love tennis!

6b My favorite things

Vocabulary interests

1 ▶95 Match the words (1–6) with the pictures (a–f). Listen and check.

comedies—movies

1 ~~comedies~~   4 detective stories
2 fish   5 pop
3 wildlife shows 6 scuba diving

a animals   b books   c 1 movies
d music   e sports f TV

2 Work in pairs. Write your favorite TV show, book, movie, and sport.
TV show—The Voice

3 Work in pairs. Ask and answer questions about the things in Exercise 2.

> Do you like TV?
>
> Yes, I do.
>
> What's your favorite TV show?
>
> The Voice.

Reading

4 Read the article about Dr. Hogan. <u>Underline</u> three interests from Exercise 1.

5 Read the article again. Are the sentences true (T) or false (F)?

1 Dr. Hogan has two jobs.   T   F
2 He's a fisherman.   T   F
3 He's from Australia.   T   F
4 His favorite place is in   T   F
   Botswana.

My favorite things: **Dr. Hogan**

▶96

Name: Dr. Zeb Hogan
Place of Birth: Arizona
Current City: Reno, Nevada
Jobs: Professor, University
of Nevada
TV presenter: Monster Fish

Grammar *he/she + like*

► HE/SHE + LIKE			
He/She		likes doesn't like	fish. cold places.
Does	he/she	like	coffee?
Yes, No,	he/she	does. doesn't.	

(doesn't = does not)

Now look at page 168.

6 Look at the grammar box. What is the negative form of *likes*? _____

7 Work in pairs. Write questions about Dr. Hogan.

1 like / fish?
Does Dr. Hogan like fish?
2 like / Botswana?
3 like / cold places?
4 like / coffee?

8 Work in pairs. Ask and answer the questions in Exercise 7.

Dr. Hogan likes fish. He loves very big fish. He isn't a fisherman. His job is to study fish in different places around the world—for example, in the Okavango Delta in Botswana. That's Dr. Hogan's favorite place. He's from a big city in Arizona. It's a very hot, dry place. Dr. Hogan doesn't like cold places very much. Does he like wet places? Well, he likes water! He loves swimming and scuba diving in his free time. He also likes wildlife shows on TV, and coffee!

Dr. Hogan catches a giant ray.

9 Work in pairs. Write five sentences about Dr. Hogan. Use *likes / doesn't like.*

He likes fish.

10 Pronunciation *likes, doesn't like*

▶ 97 Listen to five sentences about Dr. Hogan. Repeat the sentences.

Speaking *my*Life

11 Work in pairs. Look at the chart. Take turns.
Student A: Choose a person.
Student B: Ask *Does she like* questions to discover the person's identity.

> Does she like music?

> No, she doesn't.

> Does she like books?

> Yes, she does.

> Is it Teresa?

> Yes!

	Barbara	Diana	Stella	Teresa
🐾	✓	✓	✗	✗
📖	✗	✗	✓	✓
🎞	✗	✓	✗	✓
🎵	✓	✗	✓	✗
👟	✗	✓	✗	✓
📺	✓	✗	✓	✗

6c We love street food

Vocabulary food

1 Match the words with the photos.

cheese	eggs	~~fruit~~
meat	rice	vegetables

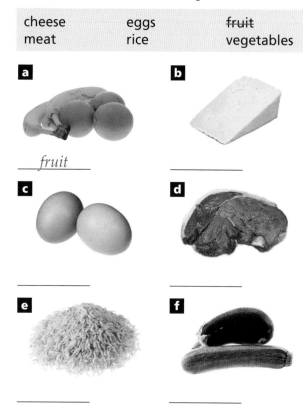

a

fruit

b

_____

c

_____

d

_____

e

_____

f

_____

2 ▶ 98 Listen and check your answers from Exercise 1. Repeat the words.

3 Work in pairs. Talk about the food you like.

Reading

4 Read the article. Match the person with the favorite food.

1 Aimee ○   ○ _soup with rice_
2 Tala ○   ○ _chicken_
3 Isko ○   ○ _spring rolls_

5 Match the meals with the correct times.

1 breakfast ○   ○ afternoon
2 dinner ○   ○ morning
3 lunch ○   ○ evening

Critical thinking what does the writer think?

6 Read paragraph 1 again. <u>Underline</u> the adjectives, like _great_ and _fantastic_. What does the writer think about street food?

Grammar object pronouns

▶ **OBJECT PRONOUNS**

Subject pronoun	Object pronoun
_I_	_me_
you	_you_
_he_	_him_
she	_her_
_it_	_it_
_we_	_us_
you	_you_
they	_them_

Now look at page 168.

7 Work in pairs. Look at the grammar box. Circle the object pronouns in the article. What does each object pronoun mean?

8 Circle the correct option.

1 I love vegetables. I have _it / them_ every day.
2 The Philippines is a great country. I love _it / them_.
3 Can I help _me / you_?
4 Where's your sister? I can't see _her / you_.
5 This is my favorite cafe. I love _her / it_.
6 Your brother is nice. I like _her / him_.

Speaking my Life

9 Work in pairs. Turn to page 157.

We love street food

▶ 99

The Philippines has great restaurants, fantastic cafes, and very good street food. You can buy lots of great food from stalls on the street. People in the Philippines love street food. Visitors to the Philippines love it, too. It's cheap, tasty, and interesting. What are people's favorite meals?

Aimee (Manila)
"I have *lechon manok* chicken for dinner every evening. I love it!"

Danilo (Tagaytay)
"I have *champorado* for breakfast. It's rice with chocolate, milk, and sugar. I have it every day."

Tala (Quezon City)
"Bananas are my favorite fruit. The food stall near my school has fantastic banana spring rolls. They're called *turon*."

Suzy (Los Angeles)
"Manila has great street food. My favorite snacks are rice cakes. I love them."

Isko (Manila)
"I have breakfast at home, but I have street food for lunch. My favorite meal is *arroz caldo*. It's soup with rice."

Let's play ping-pong

Vocabulary opinion adjectives

1 ▶ 100 Listen to three conversations. Match the words (1–4) with the four opinion adjectives (a–d).

1 sports ___
2 Felicity Jones ___
3 fish ___
4 pizza ___

a boring
b horrible
c fantastic
d great

2 Are the adjectives in Exercise 1 positive (+) or negative (-)? Write them in the chart.

Positive +	Negative -

3 Pronunciation intonation

a ▶ 101 Listen and repeat the opinions.

b Work in pairs. Make a list of four people or things. Give the list to your partner. Tell your partner your opinion of the things on his or her list.

> Basketball's boring.

> Bruno Mars is great!

Real life suggestions

4 ▶ 100 Look at the expressions for making and responding to suggestions. Listen to the conversations again. Check (✓) the expressions you hear.

> **▶ SUGGESTIONS**
>
> ☐ Let's watch soccer on TV.
> ☐ Let's go to the movie theater this weekend.
> ☐ How about pizza?
> ☐ That's a good idea.
> ☐ I love her.
> ☐ No, thanks.
> ☐ I'm sorry.
> ☐ I don't like sports very much.
> ☐ OK.

5 Add three ideas to the chart below.

Let's	go to have play watch	a burger a movie soccer pasta tennis the park _____ _____ _____	tonight. tomorrow. this weekend.
How about ...?			

6 Work in pairs. Take turns to make suggestions and respond with opinions.

7 Work in groups. Make suggestions and find an activity for this weekend.

6e Can we meet on Sunday?

Writing short messages

1 Read the messages (1–3). What is each message about? Write the number of the message.

a a celebration   _____
b a meal   _____
c a sport   _____

1 Can you come for lunch at 2 p.m. tomorrow?

2 Can I invite my sister to your party?

3 Do you like car racing? I have two tickets.

2 Match the messages in Exercise 1 with the replies (a–c).

a ☐ Yes, I love it! Thanks!

b ☐ Yes, of course you can.

c ☐ Sorry, I can't. I'm at work until 3:30.

3 Writing skill punctuation and sentence structure

a Work in pairs. Read the messages and replies in Exercises 1 and 2. Look for the punctuation below.

capital letter	A B C D
period	.
comma	,
question mark	?
exclamation mark	!

b Work in pairs. Read the sentences and add the correct punctuation.

1 we have tickets for the game tomorrow
2 yes I love their music
3 no my friend doesn't like animals
4 that television show is boring
5 thanks for the book I love it

c Look at the messages in Exercise 1. Circle the subject and underline the verbs.

1 <u>Can</u> (you) <u>come</u> for lunch at 2 p.m. tomorrow?

d Work in pairs. Write the words in order. Add the correct punctuation.

1 meet / we / tonight / can / ?
   Can we meet tonight?
2 like / french fries / you / do / ?
3 movie / this / great / is
4 like / your / does / pizza / friend / ?
5 very much / meat / like / I / don't
6 new / his / car / fantastic / is

4 Work in pairs. Write three different replies to the messages in Exercise 1.

5 Work in pairs. Write a short message. Give it to your partner. Write a reply to your partner's message.

At the market

THE
COVERED M
Fifty Quality Indepe

Helen & Douglas
House

THE
HAT
BOX

Price's
Pet
Supplies

Ben's
Cookies

NEW
TAKEAWAY
MEAL
DEAL!
3 FOR
£3.33
Any
baguette
+
Hot or
cold drink
+
Fruit or
crisps
3 FOR
£3.33

At the Covered Market in Oxford, UK

Before you watch

1 Look at the photos (1–3). Match the words (a–c) with the photos.

  a a cheese stall
  b a fish stall
  c a fruit and vegetable stall

2 Work in pairs. Which stalls in Exercise 1 do you like? Which stalls do you not like?

3 Key vocabulary

a Read the sentences. Match the **bold** words (1–4) with the pictures (a–d).

  1 I don't like fish very much—I don't like the **bones**.
  2 I love French cheese. **Camembert** is my favorite.
  3 The **tomatoes** at this fruit and vegetable stall are great.
  4 I like bananas, but I don't like **peaches**.

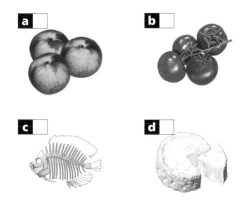

b ▶ 102 Listen and repeat the **bold** words.

4 Work in pairs. Write down things that you can buy at a market.

While you watch

5 ◻ 6 Watch the video. Work in pairs. How many things in your list from Exercise 4 are in the video?

6 ◻ 6 Watch the video again and circle the correct option.

  1 Richard Lewis loves *English cheese / French cheese / tomatoes*.

  2 Jan Szafranski likes the *cheese / fish / fruit and vegetable* stall.

  3 Amy Mills doesn't like *fruit / meat / vegetables*.

7 ◻ 6 Watch the video again. Are the sentences true (T) or false (F)?

  1 Richard teaches near the   T   F
    market.
  2 Amy lives near the market.   T   F
  3 Jan can cook fish.   T   F

8 What can you remember? Who says these sentences? Write the name of the person.

  1 My house is in this street, so this is my local market. _____
  2 My wife likes it, but I don't. It has bones. I don't like them. _____
  3 I'm a vegetarian. _____

After you watch

9 Work in pairs. Take turns to buy things.
Student A: You have a stall at the market. Decide what you sell and the prices.
Student B: Write a list. Does your partner sell your items? How much are they?

UNIT 6 REVIEW AND MEMORY BOOSTER

Grammar

1 Complete the article with the affirmative, negative, and question forms of *like*.

Jenna is a scuba diver. It's her job.
She ¹ _____ it very much. But
² _____ cold water? ³ _____
boats? And what are her interests?

Jenna, you are a professional scuba diver. Why?
Well, I ⁴ _____ swimming, and I love the ocean.

⁵ _____ **water?**
Yes. But I ⁶ _____ cold water very much.

Is this your boat?
Yes, it is. I have three boats. I ⁷ _____ big boats. They're fantastic!

And finally, what are your interests?
I ⁸ _____ sports. And I love action movies.

2 Replace the **bold** words with object pronouns.

1 Read the interview with **Jenna**.
   _____
2 Jenna loves **the ocean**. _____
3 Jenna likes **big boats**. _____
4 Jenna likes **Tom Cruise**. _____

3 ▶▶ **MB** Work in pairs. Ask and answer questions about the things in Exercise 2.

I CAN	
talk about likes and dislikes	☐
use object pronouns correctly	☐

Vocabulary

4 Cross out the item that doesn't belong.

1 chocolate   soccer   tennis
2 action movies   comedies   pop music
3 movies   meat   vegetables
4 cycling   scuba diving   wildlife shows
5 animals   basketball   fish

5 Circle the correct option.

1 I like Adele. She's *fantastic / horrible*.
2 I don't like vegetables. They're *great / horrible*.
3 I love running. It's *boring / great*.

6 ▶▶ **MB** Work in pairs. Make true sentences with the adjectives in Exercise 5.

I CAN	
talk about sports	☐
talk about food	☐
talk about interests	☐
give positive and negative opinions (adjectives)	☐

Real life

7 Read the conversation. Circle the correct option.

A: Let's ¹*have pasta / watch TV* tonight.
B: That's a good idea. What's on?
A: A movie with Eddie Redmayne.
B: No, thanks. ²*I don't like him / He's fantastic.*
A: How about Emma Stone? I have her new movie on DVD.
B: ³*No, thanks / OK. Great.* I like her a lot.

8 Work in pairs. Practice the conversation in Exercise 7.

I CAN	
give my opinion	☐
make and respond to suggestions	☐

Unit 7 Daily life

The festival of colors—the Holi festival—in Kolkata, India

FEATURES

1 Work in pairs. Look at the photo and the caption.

  1 Where are the people?   2 What is the celebration?

2 ▶ 103 Work in pairs. Listen to information about the Holi festival. Circle the correct option.

  1 The Holi festival is in *December / March*.
  2 It's a celebration of *new life / family life*.

3 ▶ 104 The Holi festival is a celebration of spring. Listen and repeat the words for the four seasons.

  spring   summer   fall   winter

4 Work in pairs. Which months are the seasons in your country?

7a Day and night

Vocabulary routines

1 ▶ 105 Listen and complete the sentences with times and places.

1 I **get up** at _____*six o'clock*_____ .
2 I **have breakfast** at _____ .
3 I **start work** at _____ .
4 I **have lunch** in a _____ .
5 I **finish work** at _____ .
6 I **have dinner** at _____ .
7 I **go to bed** at _____ .

2 Match the pictures (a–g) with the sentences (1–7) in Exercise 1.

3 Work in pairs. Write seven true or false sentences about your routines. Read the sentences to your partner. Find your partner's false sentences.

I get up at five o'clock.   False.

Reading

4 Work in pairs. Look at the photo and the caption. Where is it? What kind of class is it?

5 Work in pairs. Read about Chen Hong's routine. Is it similar to yours?

▶ 106

DAY AND NIGHT

Chen Hong's day

My name's Chen Hong. I live with my husband and parents in Shanghai. Every day, I get up at 5:30. I go to an exercise class. My husband and parents don't go to the class. After the class, I have breakfast with my friends. I start work at 8:30. At noon, I have lunch. I don't work in the afternoon. In the evening, I make dinner. We eat at eight o'clock. Then we watch TV. I go to bed at 10:30.

A morning exercise class on the Bund (riverside) in Shanghai

Grammar simple present *I/you/we/you/they*

▶ **SIMPLE PRESENT *I/YOU/WE/YOU/THEY***

| I/You/We/You/They | *eat* at eight o'clock.
don't work in the afternoon. |

Now look at page 170.

6 Look at the grammar box. What is the negative form of the simple present? Circle the negative verbs in *Day and night*.

7 ▶ 107 Complete the text about Roberto with these verbs. Listen and check.

finish	get up	go	not / go
~~have~~	have	start	work

A night in Chile

I'm Roberto. I'm married and I ¹ __*have*__ two children. I
² _____ in an observatory in Chile. I ³ _____ work
at nine o'clock at night. I ⁴ _____ work at 2:30 in the
morning and I go home and go to bed. At eight o'clock,
I ⁵ _____ and I ⁶ _____ breakfast with my wife
and children. They ⁷ _____ to school at 8:30. They
⁸ _____ to school on Saturdays and Sundays.

8 Work in pairs. Write one affirmative and one negative sentence with the **bold** verbs.

1 I **work** *at home / in a store.*
   I work at home. I don't work in a store.
2 I **go** to bed *at ten o'clock / at midnight.*
3 You **study** *English / Spanish.*
4 My friends **have** a class *at 7:30 / at 8:30.*
5 I **like** *burgers / fish.*

Grammar prepositions of time

▶ **PREPOSITIONS OF TIME**

at eight o'clock   *in* the morning

on Tuesday/Tuesdays   *at* night

Now look at page 170.

9 Look at the expressions in the grammar box. Underline similar expressions of time in the texts *Day and night* and *A night in Chile.*

10 Complete the sentences with the correct preposition.

1 They don't work __*at*__ night.
2 I don't go to school _____ the afternoon.
3 They watch TV _____ the evening.
4 We finish lunch _____ two o'clock.
5 You work _____ Saturdays.

Speaking 🔲 *my*Life

11 Work in pairs. Find things you both do at the same time. You can use some of these verbs.

eat	have	get up	go
start	study	finish	

I eat at noon.

I eat at 12:30.

We don't eat at the same time.

7b Join the club

Vocabulary hobbies

1 ▶ 108 Match the words (1–8) with the pictures (a–h). Listen and check.

1 climbing   5 reading
2 cooking   6 shopping
3 dancing   7 singing
4 painting   8 walking

2 ▶ 108 Listen again and repeat the words.

3 Work in pairs. Add your own hobbies to the list in Exercise 1.

Listening

4 ▶ 109 Listen to four people talk about their hobbies. Complete the chart.

	What?	**When?**	**Why?**
Andy	climbing	1 _____	it's exciting
Tina	2 _____	in her free time	3 it's _____
Naga	4 _____	in the evening	5 it's _____
Paul	painting	6 _____	7 it's _____

5 ▶ 110 Match the questions (1–4) with the answers (a–d). Listen and check.

1 Do you climb every day? ___
2 Do your friends sing? ___
3 Do you cook for your friends, too? ___
4 Do you paint pictures of people? ___

a No, they don't. They play the guitar and the piano.
b No, we don't. We climb on Sundays.
c Yes, I do. They love my food!
d Yes, we do.

Grammar simple present questions *I/you/we/you/they*

▶ SIMPLE PRESENT QUESTIONS *I/YOU/WE/YOU/THEY*		
Do	*I/you/we/you/they*	**listen** to music?
Yes, No,	*I/you/we/you/they*	*do.* *don't.*

Now look at page 170.

6 Work in pairs. Look at the grammar box. Then practice the questions and answers in Exercise 5.

Climbing is a popular hobby.

7 Work in pairs. Put the words in order to make questions. Then answer the questions.

1 do / you / every Saturday / climb / ?
2 enjoy / you / doing exercise / do / ?
3 you and your friends / do / go walking / ?
4 do / of your friends / you / take photos / ?
5 your parents / listen to music / do / ?
6 your friends / play ping-pong / in the evening / do / ?

8 ▶ 111 Work in pairs. Write questions with the words. Listen and check.

1 shopping (you / enjoy)
2 newspapers (you / read)
3 dancing (your friends / go)
4 basketball (you and your friends / play)
5 climbing (you / go)
6 TV (you and your friends / watch)

9 Pronunciation intonation in questions

a ▶ 111 Listen again and repeat the questions from Exercise 8.

b Work in pairs. Ask and answer the questions from Exercise 8.

Speaking *my* Life

10 Work in pairs. Add four questions about hobbies to the list in Exercise 8. Then work as a class. Ask questions. Find one person for each activity.

Do you enjoy shopping, Bruno?

Yes, I do.

7c A year in British Columbia, Canada

Vocabulary weather

1 ▶ 112 Look at the pictures. Listen and repeat the words.

cloudy ___   rainy ___   snowy ___

sunny ___   windy ___

2 ▶ 113 Listen to people from four places. Write the numbers (1–4) next to the weather words in Exercise 1.

3 Work in pairs. Describe the weather for seasons in your country.

Reading

4 Read the article. Match the paragraphs (1–4) with the photos (a–d).

5 Work in pairs. Underline the things people do in each season. Do people do the things in the article in your country?

Critical thinking finding information

6 Which words tell you about the weather in British Columbia? Find them in the passage, and write them below.

Summer: *hot, sunny*
Fall: _____
Winter: _____
Spring: _____

Grammar simple present Wh- questions

▶ SIMPLE PRESENT *WH-* QUESTIONS			
What			*do?*
Where		*I/you*	*go?*
Who	**do**	*we/you/they*	*go* with?
Why		*people*	*go* to the beach?
When			*eat?*

Now look at page 170.

7 Look at the grammar box. Circle the *Wh-* question words in the article.

8 Complete the questions with *what, where, who, why,* or *when.*

1 _____ do you go in summer?
2 _____ do you do in fall?
3 _____ do you go cycling with?
4 _____ do you like winter?

Speaking *my* Life

9 Work in pairs. What's your favorite season? Ask and answer questions. Use these ideas.
- Why / like …?
- What / do?
- When / do …?
- Where / go?
- Who / go with?

Why do you like winter?

I like to ski.

▶ 114

A YEAR IN BRITISH COLUMBIA, CANADA

SUMMER

Where do people go in summer? **1**

Summer is a great time for vacations here. The weather is hot and sunny. People go to the beach. They cook and eat outside. I go to Vancouver Island with my family. We go swimming in lakes and rivers.

FALL

What do people do in fall? **2**

In fall, classes start. Children go to school. Students go to college. It's cloudy and rainy. Trees change color from green to brown. I think it's a beautiful season.

WINTER

Where do people go in winter? **3**

In winter, it's cold, rainy, and snowy, too. A lot of people stay at home. They watch TV, read books, and cook winter food. Winter is my favorite season. I like winter sports. I go to Whistler. It's in the mountains. I go skiing and climbing.

SPRING

Why do people like spring? **4**

In spring, it's cloudy and rainy, but it isn't cold. Flowers open, birds sing, and trees are green. People go cycling and running. They meet friends and they go for walks.

7d What's the matter?

Vocabulary problems

1 ▶ 115 Look at the pictures and listen. Match the expressions you hear (1–5) with the pictures (a–e).

a ☐ bored   **b** ☐ cold   **c** ☐ hungry

d ☐ thirsty   **e** ☐ tired

2 ▶ 115 Listen again and repeat the expressions from Exercise 1.

3 Work in pairs. Tell your partner the problems in Exercise 1. Take turns.

> *I'm hungry!*

> *I'm tired!*

Real life problems

4 ▶ 116 Listen to the conversation. Write D (Dad), P (Paul), or A (Anna).

1 _____ is cold and thirsty.
2 _____ is cold and tired.
3 _____ is bored.

5 ▶ 116 Listen again. Complete the mom's suggestions.

1 Why don't you have _____ ?
2 Why don't you have _____ ?
3 Why don't you go _____ ?

▶ PROBLEMS

What's the matter?
I'm hungry/thirsty/cold/tired/hot/bored.
It's cold/hot.
I don't feel well.
I don't understand.
Why don't you have a cup of tea?

---

6 Pronunciation sentence stress

▶ 117 Listen to and repeat the three sentences. Which words are stressed?

7 Work in pairs. Look at the vocabulary in Exercise 1 and the expressions for talking about problems. Take turns to talk about problems and make suggestions.

7e Meet our club members

Writing a profile

1 Read Hans's profile. Are the sentences true (T) or false (F)?

Hans is:

1 a student.	T	F
2 married.	T	F
3 in a photography club.	T	F

2 Writing skill paragraphs

a Read Hans's profile again. Write the number of the paragraph (1–3).

_____ interests
_____ professional information
_____ family/friends

b Read the paragraphs of Jenna's profile (a–c). Put them in order (1–3).

a I live with three friends in the city. We live in a small house on a busy street. ___
b I like sports and photography. I go to sports events and take photos. ___
c I'm a student at City College. In the summer, I work at PLT Engineering. ___

c Work in pairs. Read Luther's notes. Write three paragraphs.

> a teacher   engineering
> my wife and children City College
> animals   photos

3 Make notes for your own profile. Write about:

• work/school • family/friends • interests

4 Use your notes to write three paragraphs. Check the paragraph order, spelling, and punctuation.

5 Give your profile to your partner. Find two things you have in common.

PLT Photography club
Meet our members. Come and join us!

HANS

1 I'm an engineer. I work at PLT Engineering.
2 I'm married and I have three children. We live in a small town near my company.
3 I like photography. I'm in the PLT photography club. In winter, we meet on Sundays. We go out and take photos. In summer, I go on vacation with my family. I take a lot of photos of my children and the places we go to.

JENNA

The elephants of Samburu

An elephant at night in Samburu National Reserve in Kenya

Before you watch

1 Work in pairs. Look at the photo and the caption. Where does this elephant live?

2 Key vocabulary

a Read the sentences. Match the **bold** words (1–5) with the pictures (a–e).

1 My friend has a new **jeep**. It's fast.
2 I **lie down** after lunch on Sunday.
3 Raise your **hand** if you know the answer.
4 I take a **bath** in the morning.
5 The elephant has a long **trunk**.

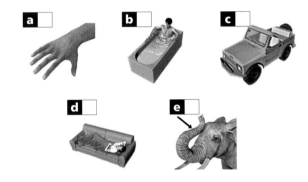

b ▶ 118 Listen and repeat the **bold** words.

3 Work in pairs. The video is about elephants in Kenya. Circle the option you think is correct.

1 Elephants live *in family groups / alone*.
2 Elephants *like / don't like* water.
3 Elephants eat *plants / animals*.

While you watch

4 ◻7 Watch the video. Check your answers from Exercise 3.

5 ◻7 Read the sentences. Watch the video again. Circle the correct option.

1 Nick Nichols is a *photographer / student*.
2 Daniel Lentipo can *speak to / identify* individual elephants.
3 Nick and Daniel follow the elephants for *four / ten* hours every day.
4 Elephants raise their trunks *to greet other elephants / when they are thirsty*.
5 Elephants *lie down / stand* to sleep.

6 ◻7 Work in pairs. Watch the video again. Write:

1 five things the elephants do every day.

2 three things Nick and Daniel do every day.

After you watch

7 Complete the text with these verbs.

drive follow get up start take walk work

Nick Nichols and Daniel Lentipo ¹ _____ at the Samburu National Reserve. They ² _____ early every day. They ³ _____ work early. They ⁴ _____ a jeep and ⁵ _____ photos of the elephants. The elephants ⁶ _____ many kilometers every day. Nick and Daniel sometimes ⁷ _____ the elephants from morning to night. Nick's photos of sleeping elephants are very beautiful.

8 Work in pairs. Ask and answer questions using these ideas.

- What / favorite animals?
- Why / like them?
- Where / live?
- What / do?

UNIT 7 REVIEW AND MEMORY BOOSTER

Grammar

1 Complete the text with the words below.

| movies | dinner | food | Friday | music |

David and Yann are brothers. They have an internet company. From Monday to
¹ _____ , they start work at seven o'clock. They finish work in the evening, and they have ² _____ at a restaurant. They like the same ³ _____ . On weekends, they don't do the same thing. David and his friends play ⁴ _____ in a band. Yann and his girlfriend go to the ⁵ _____ .

2 Work in pairs. Write questions.

1 David and Yann / brothers?
2 they / work / in the same place?
3 where / they / have dinner?
4 they / like / the same food?
5 Yann and his girlfriend / play music?

3 >> MB Work in pairs. Take turns.
Student A: Ask the questions in Exercise 2.
Student B: Answer the questions.

I CAN	
say what people do every day (simple present)	
say when people do things (prepositions of time)	

Vocabulary

4 Complete the adjectives. Write W (weather) and P (people).

1 b _ r _ d __   5 s _ n n y __
2 c l _ _ d y __   6 t h _ r s t y __
3 h _ n g r y __   7 t _ r _ d __
4 s n _ w y __   8 w _ n d y __

5 >> MB Work in pairs. Ask and answer questions with the adjectives from Exercise 4. Take turns.

> *What do you do when you're bored?*

> *I read a book.*

I CAN	
talk about the weather	
talk about problems (adjectives)	

Real life

6 Complete the sentences with the words. Then put the sentences in order (1–4) to make a conversation.

| I'm | No | What's | Why |

_____ don't you eat this pizza?   __
_____ hungry.   __
_____ , thanks—it's cold.   __
_____ the matter?   __

7 Work in pairs. Use these ideas to practice similar conversations. Take turns to start.

1 thirsty / cup of coffee
2 hot / drink some water
3 don't understand / use a dictionary

I CAN	
talk about problems	
make suggestions	

Unit 8 Work and study

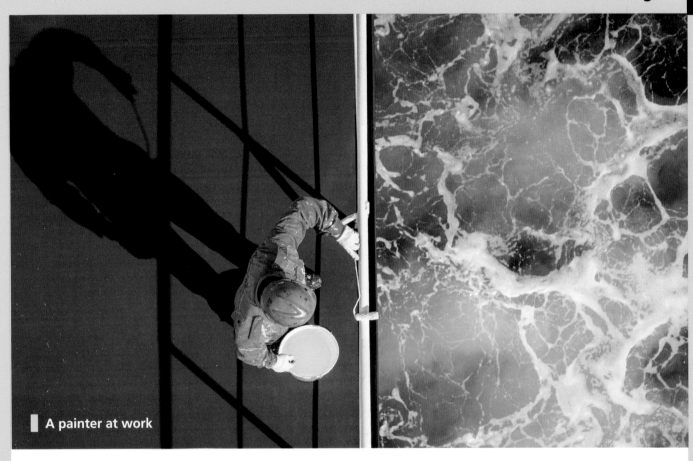

A painter at work

1 Work in pairs. Look at the photo. Where is the man?

2 ▶ 119 Listen. Circle the correct option.

1 This man's job is *in an office / outside*.
2 The man paints *houses / ships*.

3 Work in pairs. Make true sentences about these jobs. Talk about the jobs.

		inside.
Doctors		outside.
Engineers		in offices.
Painters	work	in schools.
Photographers		in hospitals.
Teachers		with people.
		with children.

What do teachers do?

Teachers work with children. They work in schools.

93

8a It's a great job!

Reading

1 Work in pairs. Look at the photo and the caption. Read the sentences. Are the sentences true (T) or false (F)?

1 The London Underground has 270 stations.   T   F

2 The London Underground is also called the Tube.   T   F

3 Parts of the London Underground aren't under the ground.   T   F

2 Read the article about Naveen and Ryan. Find these things.

1 one job   _____

2 one train line   _____

3 one station   _____

3 Read the article again. Work in pairs and answer the questions.

1 Do Naveen and Ryan like their jobs?

2 How many stations are on the Circle line?

3 Where do people buy tickets?

Grammar simple present *he/she/it*

▶ **SIMPLE PRESENT** *HE/SHE/IT*

He/She/It	**opens** the train doors. **watches** the people. **doesn't sell** tickets.

Now look at page 172.

4 Look at the grammar box. <u>Underline</u> ten simple present verbs in the article.

5 Complete the sentences about Naveen and Ryan with the correct form of the verbs.

1 Naveen _____*enjoys*_____ (enjoy) his job.

2 Naveen _____ (not / answer) people's questions.

3 Ryan _____ (not / drive) a train.

4 Ryan _____ (check) people's tickets.

5 Ryan _____ (speak) to many people.

▶ **120**

It's a **great job!**

Naveen and Ryan love their jobs. They both work on the Tube.

Naveen is a train driver. He drives a train on the Circle line. The train stops at 36 stations. Naveen opens and closes the train doors. He watches the people.

Ryan works at the Baker Street train station. He doesn't drive a train. He checks people's tickets and he answers their questions. He doesn't sell tickets—people buy them from machines.

One of the London Underground's 270 stations. Only 45 percent of the Tube is under the ground.

6 ▶ 121 Complete the paragraph about a New York subway worker. Use the correct form of the verbs. Listen and check.

not / drive	~~go~~	help
walk	watch	work

Lily [1] ___goes___ to different subway stations. She [2] _____ a train. She's a police officer. Lily [3] _____ around train stations. She [4] _____ people with problems. Sometimes, she [5] _____ in a big office. She [6] _____ the trains on computer screens.

7 Pronunciation -s and -es verb endings

a ▶ 122 Listen and repeat the sentences with these verbs. Is the s like *this* (S) or *these* (Z)?

1 enjoys ___   3 helps ___
2 goes ___   4 works ___

b ▶ 123 Look at the verbs. Listen. Check (✓) the verbs that take on an extra syllable.

☐ answer   answers
☐ drive   drives
☐ finish   finishes
☐ watch   watches

Vocabulary job activities

8 Look at these jobs. Complete the sentences with the jobs.

doctor   photographer   ~~receptionist~~

store clerk   taxi driver   waiter

1 A ___receptionist___ answers questions.
2 A _____ drives people around.
3 A _____ takes photos.
4 A _____ sells things.
5 A _____ serves food and drink.
6 A _____ helps sick people.

Speaking and writing *my*Life

9 Imagine you have one of the jobs above. Work as a class and ask questions. Write one name for each sentence.

Find a person in your class who …
enjoys his or her job.   _____
works at night.   _____
doesn't sell things.   _____
talks to people.   _____
doesn't work alone.   _____
uses a computer.   _____

Do you enjoy your job, Zoe?

Yes, I do. It's great!

10 Write six sentences using the names in Exercise 9.
Zoe enjoys her job.

8b At school

Vocabulary education

1 Look at the photo. Match four of the words with things and people in the photo.

board	book	classmate
classroom	college	notebook
pen	pencil	school
student	teacher	university

2 Write four sentences with the words in Exercise 1. Work in pairs. Take turns to read your sentences to your partner, but don't say the word. Guess your partner's word.

The name of our school is Linford High.

> The name of our ... is Linford High.

> Yes.

> School?

1 _____

2 _____

3 _____

4 _____

Kakenya Ntaiya lives in Kenya. She has her own school. It's a school for girls. The girls live at the school.

Listening

3 Look at the photo and the information Find Kakenya Ntaiya in the photo.

4 ▶ **124** Read the questions. Listen to the conversation and put the questions in order (1–4).

___ Does Kakenya work at the school?
Yes, she does. / No, she doesn't.

___ Does she teach?
Yes, she does. / No, she doesn't.

___ What does she do?
She's the head teacher / president.

_1_ Do the girls live at the school?
Yes, they do. / No, they don't.

5 ▶ **124** Listen again. Circle the correct answers to the questions in Exercise 4.

6 Work in pairs. Is this school unusual? Why or why not?

Grammar simple present questions *he/she/it*

▶ **SIMPLE PRESENT QUESTIONS** *HE/SHE/IT*

	Does	he/she the school	**teach?** **have** many students?
	Yes, No,	he/she/it	**does.** **doesn't.**
What Where	**does**	he/she	**do?** **live?**
		He/She	**'s** a teacher. **lives** in Kenya.

Now look at page 172.

7 Look at the grammar box. Complete these sentences to make questions.

1 _____ she _____ in Kenya?
(live)
2 _____ he _____ in a shop?
(work)

8 Work in pairs. Write questions about Kakenya with these words.

1 study at the school?
Does Kakenya study at the school?
2 work at the school?
3 work with girls?
4 what / do?
5 live in the United States?
6 where / live?

9 Work in pairs. Answer the questions in Exercise 8.

1 *No, she doesn't.*

10 Work in pairs. Complete the questions with *does* or *do*. Ask and answer the questions.

1 _____ boys study at Kakenya's school?
2 _____ your school have a cafe?
3 _____ your classmates live near you?
4 _____ the museum open on Saturdays?
5 _____ your class start early?

Speaking 〔*my*Life〕

11 Work in pairs.
Student A: Turn to page 154.
Student B: Turn to page 156.

8c Helping big cats

Reading

1 Work in pairs. Match the animal names (a–d) with the photos (1–4).

a leopard c ~~jaguar~~
b tiger d lion

2 Work in pairs. Do you think the sentences are true (T) or false (F)?

1 Tigers are wild animals.	T	F
2 They eat plants.	T	F
3 They live in forests.	T	F

3 Read the article and captions on page 99. Check your answers from Exercise 2.

4 Read the article again. Complete the sentences.

1 Tigers can live in both ___cold___ and _____ areas.
2 Tigers kill _____ and _____ animals.
3 Every night, Saksit checks the _____ .
4 Every month, Saksit writes a _____ .

Critical thinking asking questions

5 Work in pairs. Read the article. Write three questions about tigers. Swap questions with another pair and answer their questions. *Where do tigers live? They live in Asia.*

Grammar frequency adverbs

▶ **FREQUENCY ADVERBS**

0%				100%
never	sometimes	usually	often	always

People	**sometimes**	move into forest areas.
Tigers	**usually**	kill wild animals.

Now look at page 172.

6 Work in pairs. Look at the grammar box. Does the frequency adverb come before or after the verb in the sentence?

7 Work in pairs. Rewrite the sentences with the adverb in the correct position.

1 People kill tigers. (sometimes)
2 Tigers live in forests. (often)
3 You see wild lions in Brazil. (never)
4 I watch nature shows on TV. (always)
5 My friends go to the zoo. (often)
6 I give money to charity. (sometimes)

Speaking *my*Life

8 Make sentences 4–6 in Exercise 7 true for you. Tell your partner.

I often watch nature shows on TV.

9 Work in pairs. Ask follow-up questions to the sentences in Exercise 8.

What nature shows do you watch?

I watch a show called Earthpulse.

Why don't you watch nature shows?

I don't enjoy them.

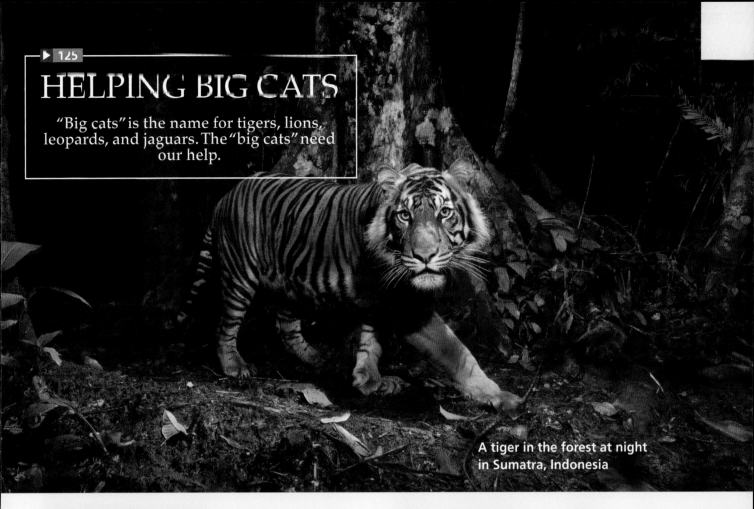

▶ 125

HELPING BIG CATS

"Big cats" is the name for tigers, lions, leopards, and jaguars. The "big cats" need our help.

A tiger in the forest at night in Sumatra, Indonesia

Tigers

number of wild tigers
in 1900 – 100,000;
in 2016 – 3,890

Tigers live in many places in Asia—from very cold mountains in the Himalayas to very hot areas. They usually live in places without people, but people sometimes move into forest areas with tigers. Tigers eat other animals. They usually kill wild animals, but they sometimes kill domestic animals. Tigers need our help because local people move into their areas and they sometimes kill the tigers.

Helping tigers

Tigers in Huai Kha
Khaeng Wildlife Park
in 1980 – 20;
in 2016 – 90

Saksit Simcharoen works at the Huai Kha Khaeng Wildlife Park in Thailand. The park is a very good place for tigers. Saksit goes into the forest every night.

Saksit Simcharoen and his team measure and put a radio collar on a tiger.

He doesn't see many tigers, but the park has 180 cameras. They take photos of the tigers, and Saksit checks the cameras. About eight of the tigers in the park have radio collars. Every month, Saksit writes a report about the tigers in the area.

8d One moment, please

Real life on the phone

1 ▶ 126 Listen to three phone calls. Who does the caller want to speak to? Write the number of the conversation (1–3).

a Mrs. Jackson ____
b Ed Smith ____
c Mr. Watts ____

2 ▶ 127 Look at the photos. Listen to two conversations again. The callers can't speak to the person. Check (✓) the reasons.

3 Look at the expressions below. Who says them: the caller (C) or the receptionist (R)?

> ### ▶ ON THE PHONE
>
> Good morning./Hello. PJ International. ____
> Can I help you? ____
> Yes, can I speak to Ed Smith, please? ____
> Yes, one moment, please. ____
> I'm sorry. He's/She's in a meeting. ____
> OK. Thank you./Thanks. ____
> I'll call back later. ____

4 ▶ 127 Complete conversation 3 with the expressions above. Listen and check.

R: ¹ _____ . City College.
   ² _____ ?
C: Yes, ³ _____
   Mrs. Jackson, please?
R: ⁴ _____ .
   She's out of the office at the moment.
C: OK. Thank you. ⁵ _____
   _____ . Goodbye.
R: Goodbye.

5 Pronunciation /s/ and /z/

▶ 128 Listen to these words. Is the *s* like *thi_s_* (S) or *the_se_* (Z)? Listen again and repeat the words.

plea_se_ ____   he'_s_ ____   ye_s_ ____

Friday_s_ ____   work_s_ ____   thank_s_ ____

works from home on Fridays

out of the office

on vacation

with a customer

on leave today

in a meeting

6 Work in pairs. Practice phone calls. Use the ideas in the photos.

> Can I speak to Paul?

> I'm sorry, he's with a customer.

8e My new job

Writing an email

1 Read Joshua's email about his new job in a call center. Complete the email with seven of these words.

calls	classmates	colleagues	job
jobs	morning	office	work

Hi!

I have a new ¹_____ ! It's great!
I ²_____ from Mondays to Fridays.
The ³_____ opens at 8 a.m. I usually
arrive at about 7:45 a.m. and I have coffee
with my ⁴_____ . They're great. We
have a meeting every ⁵_____ and the
boss gives us our ⁶_____ for the day. I
usually make about forty ⁷_____ every
day. I finish early on Fridays—let's meet for
lunch. How about next week?

Joshua

2 Read Joshua's email again. Who is it to?

a his boss   c his colleague
b his friend

3 Writing skill spelling: double letters

a Read the email again. Underline the words with double letters.

usua̲l̲ly

ar̲r̲ive

b Complete the words. Add one or two of the letters.

1 ar_____ist (t)   6 di_____icult (f)
2 busine_____ (s)   7 stu_____ent (d)
3 cla_____ca (o)   8 l___k (o)
4 co_____ege (l)   9 su_____er (m)
5 di___erent (f)   10 w_____kend (e)

c Complete the email from a student with words from Exercises 1 and 3b.

Hi!

Here I am at my new ¹_____ !
It's good! I have ²_____ every
day except Wednesdays. My
courses aren't ³_____ . I usually
do about two essays every week. I
often go out with my ⁴_____ in
the evenings. They're great. Let's
play tennis one day. How about next
⁵_____ ?

Joana

4 Write an email to a friend about a new job or course. Include a suggestion to meet.

5 Check your email. Check the spelling.

6 Work in pairs. Exchange emails. Reply to your partner's email.

8f Small ships

A ship pilot practices on a mini
ship at Port Revel.

Before you watch

1 Work in pairs. Look at the photo, title, and caption on page 102. What do you think is happening?

2 Key vocabulary

a Read the sentences. Match the **bold** words (1–4) with the pictures (a–d).

1 This **port** has a lot of ships.
2 You have to train many years to be a **ship pilot**.
3 The **waterways** are narrow.
4 The **waves** at the beach are very big.

b ▶ 129 Listen and repeat the **bold** words.

While you watch

3 🎥 8 Watch the video. Check your answers for Exercise 1.

4 🎥 8 Test your memory. Circle the correct option. Watch the video and check your answers.

1 Port Revel is in *Italy / Argentina / France*.
2 Port Revel ships are *10 / 25 / 75* times smaller than real ships.
3 Port Revel gets about *100 / 200 / 300* students every year.

4 Most of Port Revel's students are *ship builders / ship pilots / engineers*.
5 The ship pilots in the class are from Russia, Brazil, and *Spain / Cambodia / Canada*.

After you watch

5 How often do these things happen? Circle the correct frequency adverb.

1 At Port Revel, people _____ practice on real ships.
  a never
  b sometimes
2 Port Revel _____ trains ship pilots.
  a usually
  b always
3 The ship pilots _____ practice together.
  a never
  b sometimes
4 Arthur de Graauw _____ asks ship captains to test his mini ships.
  a never
  b often

6 Work in pairs.
Student A: Imagine you are a ship pilot.
Student B: Imagine you build mini ships at Port Revel.
Ask and answer the questions below. Try to use frequency adverbs in your answers.

- Where do you work?
- What do you usually do in your job?
- Do you like your job? Why or why not?

7 Work in groups. Tell each other your partner's answers from Exercise 6.

> Nora is a ship pilot.
> She works in France.

UNIT 8 REVIEW AND MEMORY BOOSTER

Grammar

1 Work in pairs. Read about Joel. Write six sentences about him with the **bold** words. Use *he*.

Hi. I'm Joel. I'm 46. ¹ I live in **New Mexico**. I'm a truck driver. ² I have a **new job**. In my new job, ³ I drive **from New Mexico to Texas** every week. That's about 2,400 kilometers. ⁴ I stop **every four hours** for a break. ⁵ I sleep in my **truck**. ⁶ In the evenings, I meet other drivers at **diners**.

2 Rewrite sentences 4, 5, and 6 with these frequency adverbs.

4 usually   5 often   6 sometimes

3 Write questions about Joel with these words.

1 What / do?
2 How often / stop?
3 Who / meet?

4 ≫ MB Work in pairs. Take turns.
Student A: Ask the questions in Exercise 3.
Student B: Answer the questions.

I CAN	
talk about what people do (simple present)	
say how often people do things (frequency adverbs)	

Vocabulary

5 Read the sentences. Write the job.

1 They take photos.   _____
2 They drive people.   _____
3 They help sick people.   _____
4 They answer questions
  on the phone.   _____
5 They serve drinks.   _____
6 They sell things to
  customers.   _____

6 ≫ MB Match the jobs (1–6) from Exercise 5 with these places (a–f).

a in a store ____   d in a hospital ____
b in an office ____   e in a car   ____
c in a cafe ____   f outside   _1_

7 Complete the words about education.

1 People: classmate, s t _ _ _ _ _ _,
  t e _ _ _ _ _ _
2 Places: college, u n _ _ _ _ _ _ _ _ _,
  s c _ _ _ _ _, c l _ _ _ _ _ _ _

I CAN	
talk about jobs and job activities	
talk about education	

Real life

8 Put the phone conversation in order (1–6).

____ Can I speak to her assistant?
____ Hello. Can I speak to **Ms. Becker**, please?
____ I'm sorry. **She's on vacation.**
_1_ Good morning, **Sports Unlimited**.
____ OK. Thank you.
____ Yes, one moment please.

9 Work in pairs. Practice the conversation in Exercise 8. Change the **bold** words.

I CAN	
make phone calls	

Unit 9 Travel

A passenger shows her passport and train ticket at the Machu Picchu village train station, Peru.

1 Work in pairs. Look at the photo. Where are the people?

2 ▶ 130 Listen to four people talk about travel. Match the speakers (1–4) with the pictures.

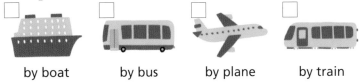

by boat   by bus   by plane   by train

3 ▶ 130 Listen again. Work in pairs. Where do the people go? When do they go?

4 Work in pairs. Ask and answer questions about travel with *where, when,* and *how.*

I usually travel in July.

Where do you go?

I go to Moscow and Kiev.

9a Ready to go

Vocabulary clothes

1 ▶ **131** Look at the photos. Listen and repeat the words.

a pair of boots

a hat

a coat

a top

a jacket

a T-shirt

a skirt

a pair of jeans

a dress

a pair of shoes

a shirt

a pair of pants

a scarf

a pair of shorts

a sweater

2 Work in pairs. Look at your classmates. Talk about their clothes. Guess their names.

> *A white shirt and black pants.*

> *Ramon?*

3 Work in pairs. Talk about your clothes. What do you usually wear

- for work?
- at college?
- on weekends?
- on vacation?

> *I usually wear a dress for work.*

Reading and listening

4 Read the article by Kate Renshaw. <u>Underline</u> the clothes.

5 Read the article again. Work in pairs. What does Kate take with her? What does her sister take?

▶ **132**

by Kate Renshaw

Ready to go

I'm a travel writer. I usually travel alone. With my passport, money, and phone, I'm ready. I take a very small suitcase. But when my family comes with me, there are lots of bags. For example, my sister always has two big suitcases. In my sister's suitcases, there are three jackets, lots of sweaters, seven pairs of pants, and lots of tops. There are books, too. She never travels without books. In my husband's bag, there's a pair of boots and there are three pairs of shoes! How many pairs of shoes does one man need?

6 ▶ 133 Listen to Kate talk about her next trip. Check (✓) the things that are in her suitcase.

☐ a camera   ☐ some books
☐ a laptop   ☐ a dress
☐ two shirts ☐ a pair of shoes
☐ shorts   ☐ some T-shirts

Grammar *there is/are*

▶ THERE IS/ARE			
There's	a	laptop	*in my suitcase.*
There are	two	shirts	
	some	T-shirts	
(there's = there is)			

Now look at page 174.

Two families with their bags on a trip to Santa Cruz Island, California

7 Look at the grammar box. Then look at these sentences. Circle the correct option.

1 We use *there's / there are* with singular nouns.
2 We use *there's / there are* with plural nouns.

8 Work in pairs. Write sentences with *there's* and *there are*, and the things in Exercise 6.

There are some T-shirts in Kate's suitcase.

9 Pronunciation *there are*

a ▶ 134 Listen and repeat the sentences with *there are*. Is the word *are* stressed?

b Work in pairs. Take turns to say true or false sentences about the photo.

There are three children.

False. There are two children.

10 Complete the sentences with *there's* or *there are*. Add extra words or numbers so that the sentences are true for you.

1 _____ a phone _____ .
2 _____ _____ people in this class.
3 _____ _____ desks in this room.
4 _____ a book on my desk.
5 _____ a board in this classroom.

Speaking myLife

11 Work in pairs. Choose a place you travel to a lot. What do you take with you? Write a list. Tell your partner where you go and what you usually have in your suitcase. Use *there's* and *there are*.

I often go to Ecuador. In my suitcase, there are usually four T-shirts. There's a …

9b Places to stay

Vocabulary hotel rooms

1 ▶ 135 Look at the photos (1–9). Then listen and repeat the words. Match the words and the photos.

bathtub	bed	chair
fridge	desk	lamp
shower	couch	TV

1 _____

2 _____

3 _____

4 _____

5 _____

6 _____

7 _____

8 _____

9 _____

2 Work in pairs. Which things are always in a hotel room? Which things are usually in a hotel room?

> *There's always a bed.*

> *There's usually a fridge.*

Listening

3 Work in pairs. Look at the photo below. Who do you think stays in this kind of hotel?

| families | business travelers |
| students | young couples |

4 ▶ 136 Listen to Sandra and Lucia plan their trip to Cape Town. Do they want a cheap hotel or an expensive hotel?

_____

5 ▶ 136 Listen again. Read Lucia's questions and circle the words she uses.

1 Are there any hotels near the *airport / beach*?
2 Is there a cheap hotel *in the city center / near the airport*?
3 Is there a *bus / train* to the city center?

The Cape Grace Hotel, Cape Town, South Africa

Grammar *there is/are* negative and question forms

▶ *THERE IS/ARE* NEGATIVE and QUESTION FORMS

There **isn't**	a train.	
There **aren't**	**any** cheap hotels.	
Is there	a cheap hotel?	Yes, there **is**. No, there **isn't**.
Are there	**any** hotels?	Yes, there **are**. No, there **aren't**.

Now look at page 174.

6 Look at the grammar box. Then look at these sentences. Circle the correct option.
1 Use *a / any* after **there isn't** and **Is there**.
2 Use *a / any* after **there aren't** and **Are there**.

7 Complete the sentences and questions with *a* or *any*.
1 Are there _____ taxis?
2 Is there _____ TV?
3 There aren't _____ trains at night.
4 Is there _____ shower or _____ bathtub?
5 Are there _____ people at the cafe?

8 Work in pairs. Put the words in order to make questions and negative sentences.
1 drinks / are / in the fridge / any / there / ?
Are there any drinks in the fridge?
2 in the room / aren't / chairs / there / any / .
3 a couch / there / in our room / is / ?
4 near / an airport / there / the beach / isn't / .
5 a train / there / the airport / is / from / ?
6 there / beaches / near / any / the hotel / are / ?

Speaking and writing my Life

9 Work in pairs. Tell your partner the name of your hometown or a place you know. Write questions about your partner's place. Use *Is there a/an*, or *Are there any*.

airport nice beach cheap restaurants expensive hotels good hotels tourist attractions	in near	the city the town the city center

10 Work in pairs. Ask and answer your questions from Exercise 9.

> *Are there any good hotels near the city center?*

> *Yes, there are. There are some four-star hotels and some five-star hotels.*

11 Work in pairs. Write true sentences with the information from Exercise 10. Use affirmative and negative forms.

12 Work in pairs.
Student A: Turn to page 154.
Student B: Turn to page 156.

9c Across a continent

Reading

1 Work in pairs. Look at the map and the photos on page 111. What things do you think you can see or do on a trip across Russia?

2 Read the article on page 111 and check your ideas from Exercise 1.

3 Read the article again. Are the sentences true (T) or false (F)?

1	There's a road from Moscow to Vladivostok.	T	F
2	You can leave the train and visit the cities.	T	F
3	There are eight towns near Lake Baikal.	T	F
4	The Trans-Siberian Highway ends in Novosibirsk.	T	F

Critical thinking who is it for?

4 Work in pairs. Where do you think the article is from (e.g., a newspaper, a magazine)? Who do you think it is for (e.g., Russians, tourists, tour guides)?

Vocabulary travel

5 Match the verbs with the words. Then check your answers in the article.

1 buy   a bus
2 take   by train
3 travel   cities
4 visit   tickets

6 Complete the questions with verbs from Exercise 5. Work in pairs. Ask and answer the questions.

1 How often do you _____ by train?
2 Do you usually _____ tickets online?
3 How often do you _____ different cities?
4 Do you often _____ a bus to work?

Grammar imperative forms

> ▶ IMPERATIVE FORMS
>
> **Buy** your tickets before your trip.
> **Don't wait** until you get to Moscow.
> (don't = do not)
>
> ───────────────────────────
>
> Now look at page 174.

7 Look at the grammar box. Are the words in **bold** nouns or verbs? _____

8 Give tips to a traveler in Russia. Complete the sentences with the base forms of verbs. Use verbs from the article on page 111.

1 _____ non-stop in seven days.
2 _____ to other passengers.
3 _____ some words in Russian.
4 _____ in hotels.
5 _____ the big cities.
6 _____ by the Trans-Siberian Highway.

Writing and speaking myLife

9 Work in pairs. Write five tips for travelers in your country. Think of reasons for the tips. *Don't travel by bus.*

10 Work in groups of four. Discuss your tips. Ask follow-up questions.

> Don't travel by bus.

> Why?

> The buses are very slow.

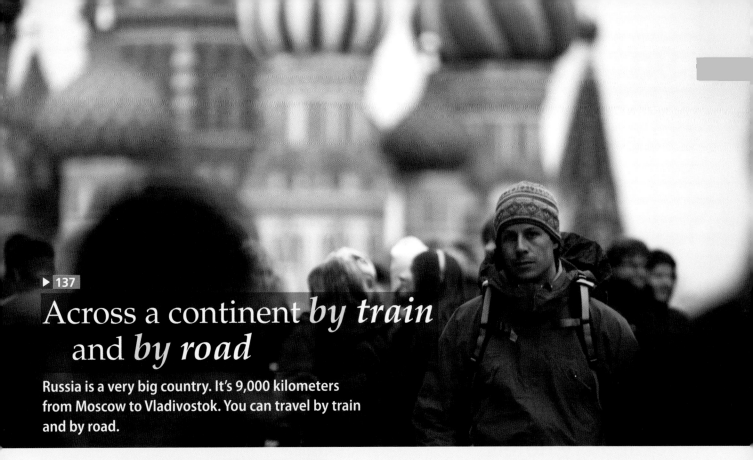

▶ 137

Across a continent *by train* and *by road*

Russia is a very big country. It's 9,000 kilometers from Moscow to Vladivostok. You can travel by train and by road.

BY TRAIN: THE TRANS-SIBERIAN RAILWAY

Trains leave Moscow almost every day. Buy your tickets before your trip—don't wait until you get to Moscow. There are two kinds of trips:

You can travel non-stop in seven days. You sleep and eat on the train. You can talk to other passengers. You can learn some words in Russian. You can look at beautiful views.

You can stop and stay in hotels. You can visit the big cities. In Novosibirsk—the main city in Siberia—there are interesting museums, art galleries, and theaters. There's also a famous opera house. From the towns of Irkutsk or Ulan-Ude, you can take a bus or train to Lake Baikal. This is a UNESCO World Heritage site. Lake Baikal is 636 kilometers long. There are only four or five towns near it. The lake is a great place for sports activities.

BY ROAD: THE TRANS-SIBERIAN HIGHWAY

Do you like exciting trips? Then go by the Trans-Siberian Highway. Some people drive cars and some people travel with Russian drivers.

When you finally get to Vladivostok, you can fly home or continue your journey—there's a boat from Vladivostok to Japan every week.

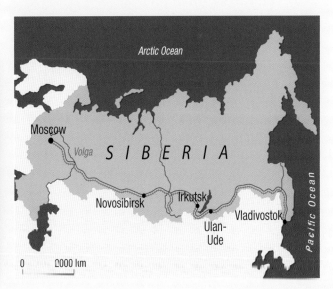

9d At the hotel

Vocabulary hotels

1 Complete the sentences with these words.

cafe	gift shop	parking lot
pool	restaurant	Wi-Fi

1 You can have dinner in the _____ .
2 You can go online with _____ .
3 You can buy gifts in the _____ .
4 You can have a sandwich at the
   _____ .
5 You can park your car in the _____ .
6 You can swim in the _____ .

Real life requests

2 ▶ 138 Listen to a conversation between a
receptionist and two hotel guests. Write:

1 the number of nights
   _____

2 the room number
   _____

3 the restaurant opening hours
   _____

4 the Wi-Fi password
   _____

3 ▶ 138 Listen again. Match the requests
(1–4) with the responses (a–d).

1 I have a reservation for two nights. ___
2 Can I have your name, please? And a
   credit card? ___
3 I'd like help with these bags. ___
4 Can you tell me the Wi-Fi password? ___

a That's no problem.
b Certainly.
c Of course.
d Here you are.

▶ REQUESTS

I have a reservation for two nights.
I'd like help with these bags.
Can I have your name, please?
Can you call a taxi, please?
Certainly.
Here you are.
Of course.
That's no problem.

4 Look at the expressions for requests. Work
in pairs. Which question is a request for
information?

5 Pronunciation *I'd like, We'd like*

a ▶ 139 Listen and repeat the sentences.

b Work in pairs. Practice these requests.
Use *I'd like* or *We'd like*.

a different room
lunch in our room
the key for our room
a taxi to the airport

*I'd like a
different room.*   *That's no problem.*

6 Work in groups of three. Look at track 138
of the audioscript on page 187. Practice
the conversation.

9e A great place to visit

Writing travel advice

1 Work in pairs. Read the advice on a travel website. Answer the questions.

1 What's the name of the city?
2 How can you travel there?
3 Where can you eat?
4 What can you eat?
5 What can you see?
6 What can you do?

2 Read the advice again. <u>Underline</u> four tips from Dani.

3 Writing skill *because*

a Work in pairs. Find three sentences with the word *because*.

b Work in pairs. Rewrite these sentences with *because*.

1 Go in spring. It's very hot in summer.
2 Travel by bus. It's cheap.
3 Choose your hotel in advance. It's a very popular place.

4 Make notes about a place you know. Use the questions in Exercise 1.

5 Use your notes and write two or three paragraphs of advice for travelers to the place. Include at least one tip.

6 Check your advice. Check the spelling, punctuation, and verbs.

7 Work in pairs. Exchange advice. Is your partner's place a good place to travel to?

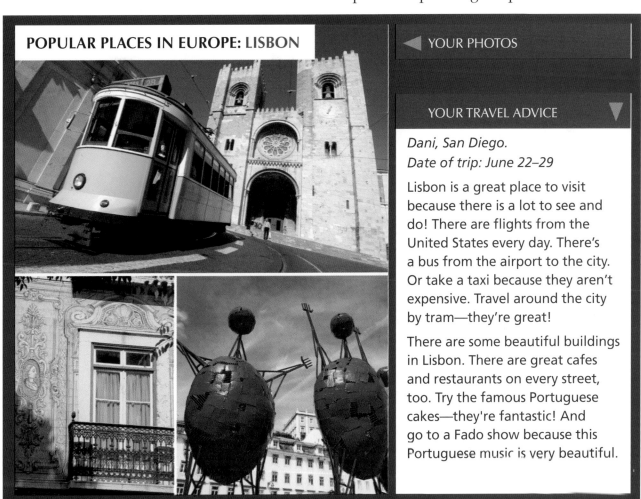

POPULAR PLACES IN EUROPE: LISBON

◀ YOUR PHOTOS

YOUR TRAVEL ADVICE ▼

Dani, San Diego.
Date of trip: June 22–29

Lisbon is a great place to visit because there is a lot to see and do! There are flights from the United States every day. There's a bus from the airport to the city. Or take a taxi because they aren't expensive. Travel around the city by tram—they're great!

There are some beautiful buildings in Lisbon. There are great cafes and restaurants on every street, too. Try the famous Portuguese cakes—they're fantastic! And go to a Fado show because this Portuguese music is very beautiful.

The people of the reindeer

A Sami man with his reindeer

Before you watch

1 Look at the photo on page 114. What are the animals? __ _____

2 Work in pairs. Look at the map. Which continent is this?

3 Read about the Sami people. Work in pairs. Answer the questions.

1 Where do they live?
2 What does *eallin* mean?

The people of the reindeer

The Sami people live in Norway, Sweden, Finland, and Russia. They are the "people of the reindeer." Traditional Sami people move from place to place with their animals. When they travel, they live in tents. Reindeer are very important to the Sami people. In the Sami language, the word for "a group of reindeer" is *eallu* and the word for "life" is *eallin*.

4 Key vocabulary

a Read the sentences. Match the **bold** words (1–3) with the pictures (a–c).

1 **Cut** the cake in two. __
2 This chair is **hard**. __
3 I like this. It's **soft**. __

b ▶ 140 Listen and repeat the **bold** words.

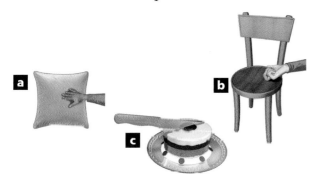

While you watch

5 🎥 9 These sentences describe scenes in the video. Watch the video and put the scenes in order (1–6).

__ A man sits with his dog.
__ A man cuts a piece of bread.
_1_ There's a person in a tent.
__ A woman works near a house.
__ A young child laughs.
__ A young couple sits in a room.

6 🎥 9 Watch the video again. Read these sentences about the Sami. Are the sentences true (T) or false (F)?

1 The Sami people travel with their reindeer in winter. T F
2 When they travel, the Sami people live in tents. T F
3 Some young people wear traditional clothes. T F
4 The children travel with the reindeer. T F
5 Hard snow is good for the reindeer. T F
6 The Sami people have dogs. T F

After you watch

7 Work in pairs. What does the man with the dog say?

8 Work in pairs. Complete the sentences about the Sami people with your own words.

1 The Sami are from …
2 They travel …
3 On the journey, …

9 Work as a class. Do you think the Sami way of life is easy or difficult? Why?

UNIT 9 REVIEW AND MEMORY BOOSTER

Grammar

1 Look at the photo. Complete the questions with *Is there / Are there*.

1 _____ a map?
2 _____ a scarf?
3 _____ any books?
4 _____ a hat?
5 _____ a camera?

2 Work in pairs. Ask and answer the questions in Exercise 1. Take turns.

3 ≫ MB Work in pairs. Look at the photo for ten seconds. Test your memory. Take turns.
Student A: Read a sentence aloud.
Student B: Say true or false.

1 There's a laptop.
2 There's a water bottle.
3 There are sunglasses.
4 There are boots.
5 There's money.

4 Work in pairs. Put the words in order to write tips.

1 early / the / buy / tickets
2 night / travel / don't / at
3 cafes / try / local / the
4 stay / hotel / this / don't / in

I CAN	
use *there is* and *there are* correctly	
give tips (imperative forms)	

Vocabulary

5 Which clothes are not right? Cross the odd ones out.

1 In cold weather, I wear ~~A pair of shorts~~ / a coat / a pair of boots / a hat.
2 In hot weather, I wear a T-shirt / a pair of shorts / a skirt / a jacket.
3 In the office, I wear a pair of pants / a hat / a shirt / a pair of shoes.

6 ≫ MB Work in pairs. Talk about what you wear every day.

7 Put the letters in order to make words for things in a hotel room.
1 r i h c a   _____
2 m l p a   _____
3 r o h s w e   _____
4 h u o c c   _____

I CAN	
talk about clothes	
talk about hotel rooms	

Real life

8 Complete the hotel requests (1–4). Then match the requests with the responses (a–d).

1 We'd like a _____ for tonight.   ___
2 I'd like help with my _____ .   ___
3 Can you tell me the Wi-Fi _____ ?   ___
4 Can you _____ a taxi?   ___

a Yes, of course. What time do you want it?
b Here you are. It's on this card.
c That's no problem. What are your names?
d Certainly, sir. Just one moment.

9 Work in pairs. Practice the exchanges in Exercise 8.

I CAN	
make and respond to requests	
talk about traveling	

Unit 10 Famous people

Ayrton Senna
in 1994

FEATURES

1 ▶ 141 Work in pairs. Look at the photo of Ayrton Senna. Do you know his job and nationality? Listen and check.

2 ▶ 142 Listen and repeat the years. Match the years with the people.

1879–1955	○	○ Ayrton Senna
1918–2013	○	○ John Lennon
1940–1980	○	○ Isabel Allende
1942–present	○	○ Malala Yousafzai
1960–1994	○	⊙ Albert Einstein
1997–present	○	○ Nelson Mandela

3 ▶ 143 Listen and check your answers from Exercise 2.

4 Work in pairs. Choose and write five important years in a list. Dictate these years to your partner. Then compare your lists.

10a Famous firsts

Reading

1 Work in pairs. Look at the photos below. What do the people have in common?

2 ▶ 144 Read the *Explorers* quiz below. Complete the sentences with the names. Listen and check.

Grammar *be: was/were*

▶ BE: WAS/WERE

I/He/She/It	**was**	an explorer. Russian.
You/We/You/They	**were**	from Russia.

Now look at page 176.

3 Look at the grammar box. <u>Underline</u> the past forms of *be* in the paragraphs (1–4). Then match the paragraphs with four people in the quiz.

1 She was born in **1939**. She was in a team of Japanese mountaineers. They were all women.

2 He was born in **1480**. He was Portuguese, but he was an explorer for the Spanish king Carlos I.

3 She was born in the United States on **September 29th, 1955**. She was the leader of an expedition to the South Pole in **1993**. All the people on the expedition were women.

4 He was from Norway and he was born on **July 16th, 1872**. His parents were rich. His father was a sea captain.

Explorers

Ferdinand Magellan

Yuri Gagarin

Roald Amundsen

Junko Tabei

Ann Bancroft

Valentina Tereshkova

Do you know these famous explorers? Match their names with the expeditions.

- The first around-the-world expedition was from 1519 to 1522. The expedition captain was _____ .

- The first successful South Pole expedition was in 1911. The expedition leader was _____ .

- The first man in space was _____ . The first woman in space was _____ . They were both from Russia.

- The first woman at the top of Everest was _____ on May 16th, 1975.

- The first woman at the North Pole was _____ on May 1st, 1986.

4 Circle the correct option.

1 I *was* / *were* born in Kuala Lumpur.
2 My parents *was* / *were* born in Texas.
3 My father *was* / *were* born in 1970.

5 Complete the paragraphs with *was* and *were*.

Yuri Gagarin [1] _____ born in 1934. His parents [2] _____ farmers. From 1955 to 1961, he [3] _____ a pilot. The first space rockets [4] _____ small and so the first people in space [5] _____ small, too. Gagarin [6] _____ a small man—1.57 meters tall.

Valentina Tereshkova [7] _____ born in Central Russia in 1937. Her parents [8] _____ from Belarus. She [9] _____ a factory worker.

After their trips into space in 1961 and 1963, Gagarin and Tereshkova [10] _____ famous all over the world.

6 Pronunciation *was/were* weak forms

a ▶ 145 Listen and repeat three sentences from Exercise 5.

b Work in pairs. Write three *was/were* sentences about Valentina Tereshkova. Read them to your partner.

Vocabulary dates

7 Look at the chart below. Complete the dates with information from the *Explorers* quiz.

Important dates in exploration	
_____ **1st**, _____	first woman at the North Pole
2nd	
November **3rd**, 1957	Sputnik II into space
October **4th**, 1957	Sputnik I into space
5th / **6th** / **7th** / **8th** / **9th** / **10th** / **11th**	
April **12th**, 1961	first man in space
December **13th**, 1972	last man on the moon
December **14th**, 1911	first people at the South Pole
15th	
_____ **16th**, _____	first woman at the top of Everest
17th / **18th** / **19th**	
July **20th**, 1969	first men on the moon

8 ▶ 146 Look at the chart again. Listen and repeat the ordinal numbers.

9 ▶ 147 Listen and repeat the dates.

May first, 1986.

10 Work in pairs. Look at the chart in Exercise 7. Take turns.
Student A: Say a date.
Student B: Say the event.

May 1st, 1986.

The first woman at the North Pole.

11 ▶ 148 Say these ordinal numbers. Listen and check.

21st	22nd	23rd	24th
25th	26th	27th	28th
29th	30th	31st	

Speaking myLife

12 Work in pairs. What are three important dates in your country?

July 4th is Independence Day.

13 Work in pairs. Write three important dates from your past. Show them to your partner. Take turns.
Student A: Say your partner's dates.
Student B: Say why the dates are important.

September 1st, 1990.

It was my first day at school.

10b People I remember

Listening

1 Work in pairs. Who was your best friend when you were young? Is he or she your best friend now?

2 Work in pairs. Read the information about the radio show. Answer the questions.

1 When's the show on the radio?
2 What's the show about?
3 Who's on the show today?

3 ▶ 149 Listen to Joe and Aneta. Complete the sentences with these words.

| a writer | animals | *Frankenstein* | meerkats |
| on TV | reading | | |

1 Joe loves _____ .
2 David Attenborough was _____ .
3 Joe's favorite show was about _____ .
4 Aneta loves _____ .
5 Mary Shelley was _____ .
6 _____ was by Mary Shelley.

4 ▶ 149 Listen again. Circle the correct answer to the interviewer's questions.

1 Was he on TV?
Yes, he was. / No, he wasn't.
2 Were the shows only for children?
Yes, they were. / No, they weren't.
3 Were you good at English?
Yes, I was. / No, I wasn't.

5 Work in pairs. What were you good at in school? Ask and answer questions.

> Were you good at English in school?

> Yes, I was.

People I remember

Radio 6, 7:30 p.m., March 13th

On today's show, we remember people who were important to us when we were young. We talk to Joe, Aneta, and Olga about a TV star, a writer, and an Olympic champion.

David Attenborough and some meerkats

Grammar be: was/were negative and question forms

▶ **BE: WAS/WERE NEGATIVE and QUESTION FORMS**

I/He/She/It You/We/You/They	wasn't weren't	on TV. famous.
Was **Were**	I/he/she/it you/we/you/they	on TV? famous?

Yes, No, Yes, No,	I/he/she/it I/he/she/it you/we/you/they you/we/you/they	**was.** **wasn't.** **were.** **weren't.**

Now look at page 176.

6 Work in pairs. Look at the grammar box. What are the negative and question forms of *was* and *were*?

7 ▶ 150 Complete the interview with Olga with *was*, *were*, *wasn't*, or *weren't*. Listen and check.

I: Olga, who [1] ___was___ important to you when you were young?

O: I remember Michael Johnson. He was a great athlete.

I: [2] _____ he an Olympic champion?

O: Yes, he [3] _____ . Four times. The last time was in 2000.

I: [4] _____ the 2000 Olympic Games in Beijing?

O: No, they [5] _____ . They were in Sydney.

I: [6] _____ you good at sports in school?

O: No, I [7] _____ .

8 Complete the questions with *was* or *were*.

1 ___Were___ you born in this country?
2 _____ your parents famous?
3 _____ you happy at school?
4 _____ your teachers at school nice?
5 _____ your school good?

9 Work in pairs. Ask and answer the questions in Exercise 8.

Vocabulary describing people

10 Work in pairs. Look at the **bold** words below. Think of a person you both know for each word.

1 A **famous** actor   *Meryl Streep*
2 A **funny** person   *Mr. Bean*
3 A **popular** person who has lots of friends
4 A **nice** person who helps other people
5 An **interesting** person who has lots of ideas

Speaking myLife

11 Work in groups. Who was important to you when you were young? Write three names. Think about the answers to these questions.

• Who was he/she?
• Why was he/she important to you?

12 Work in groups. Take turns. Read out your names from Exercise 11. Ask and answer questions about the names.

Who was
Monika Gomes?

She was my first teacher.
She was funny and nice.

10c The first Americans

Reading

1 Work in pairs. Do you think these sentences are true (T) or false (F)?

1 The Inca Empire was in   T   F
  North America.
2 The Maya people were from   T   F
  Central America.
3 The Aztecs were from Peru.   T   F
4 The Apache people were from T   F
  South America.

2 Read the first paragraph of *The first Americans*. Check your answers from Exercise 1.

3 Read the rest of the article. <u>Underline</u>:

1 one thing the Incas were famous for.
2 two things the Maya people were famous for.
3 two Aztec words we use in English.
4 a famous Apache.

4 Can you remember? Complete the sentences. Then check your answers in the article.

1 There are _____ countries in North, Central, and South America.
2 The Inca roads were on the _____ coast of South America.
3 The Mayan "one" was a _____ .

5 Work in pairs. Who were important leaders in your country's history?

Grammar regular simple past verbs

▶ **REGULAR SIMPLE PAST VERBS**

I/You He/She/It We/You/They	**lived** in Central America. **died** in 1903.

Now look at page 176.

6 Look at the grammar box. Work in pairs. What are the base forms of the verbs? What letter do we add to make the simple past form?

7 Work in pairs. Complete the sentences.

lived	was born	died

1 Albert Einstein *was born* in Germany in 1879. He _____ in 1955.
2 Isabel Allende _____ in Peru in 1940. She _____ in Chile for many years.
3 Malala Yousafzai _____ in Pakistan in 1997.

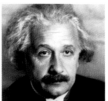  

Albert Einstein   Isabel Allende   Malala Yousafzai

Critical thinking making a timeline

8 Work in pairs. Look at Exercise 2 on page 117. Write the information about the six people's lives on a timeline.

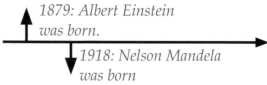

1879: Albert Einstein was born.

1918: Nelson Mandela was born

Speaking my Life

9 Work in pairs. Choose four famous people. Find out when and where they were born, lived, and died. Why were they famous?

10 Work with a new partner. Take turns. Give details of your famous people. Can you guess your partner's people?

THE FIRST AMERICANS

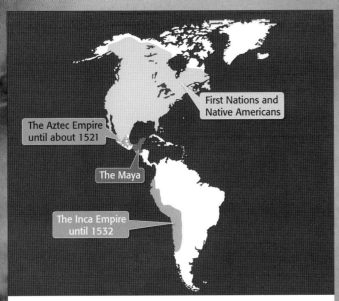

First Nations and Native Americans

The Aztec Empire until about 1521

The Maya

The Inca Empire until 1532

Geronimo: Apache hero
June 16th, 1829–February 17th, 1909

There are now twenty-three countries and twenty-three nationalities in North, Central, and South America. In the past, there were different groups of people in America. The Inca people lived in a large area of South America. The Maya people lived in Central America. And people in Mexico were part of the Aztec Empire. In North America, the Apache, the Navajo, the Sioux, and other Native American groups lived in different areas.

The Inca Empire was famous for its roads. There were roads on the west coast of South America, from the north to the south. The Maya people were famous for their writing and math systems. In Mayan math, a dot was "one" and a bar was "five." The capital city of the Aztecs was Tenochtitlan. Mexico City is in the same place. The words *chocolate* and *tomato* were Aztec words.

Famous rulers in South America were Tupac Amaru, an Inca ruler, and Moctezuma, an Aztec ruler. One famous Apache was Geronimo, but he wasn't a ruler. Geronimo was born on June 16th, 1829. When he was a young man, there was a war between the US government and Native Americans. Geronimo was a war hero. He died in 1909.

10d I'm sorry

Vocabulary activities

1 Look at the photos. Match the words (1–6) with the photos (a–f).

At nine o'clock yesterday morning, I was …

1 on a train   4 in traffic
2 at home   5 not well
3 busy   6 on the phone

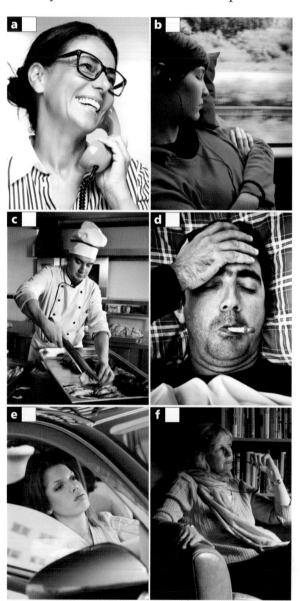

a

b

c

d

e

f

Real life apologizing

2 ▶ 152 Listen to three conversations. Write the number of the conversation (1–3) next to the places.

a in a cafe ____
b in a classroom ____
c in an office ____

3 ▶ 152 Look at the expressions for apologizing. Listen for these expressions in the conversations.

> **▶ APOLOGIZING**
>
> I'm (very) sorry.   We weren't at home.
> I'm sorry I'm late.   It's OK.
> The train was late.   That's OK.
> I was (very) busy.   Don't worry.

4 Pronunciation sentence stress

a ▶ 153 Listen and repeat these sentences. Underline the word with the main stress.

1 I'm sorry I'm late.
2 The train was late.
3 I was very busy.
4 We weren't at home.

b Work in pairs. Look at track 152 of the audioscript on page 188. Practice the conversations. Pay attention to sentence stress.

5 Work in pairs. Practice the expressions for apologizing. Use the vocabulary in Exercise 1.

Hello.

Hi. I'm sorry I'm late. I was in traffic.

10e Sorry!

Writing an email

1 Read the emails (1–3). Which two are apologies (A)? Which one expresses sympathy (S)? Write your answers on the emails below.

2 Read the emails again. Answer the questions.

1 Where was Marc yesterday? _____
2 Who was sick last week? _____
3 What information does Ms. Braun need? _____

1

> Hi Jen,
>
> I'm very sorry about yesterday. I was very busy at work. I had meetings all day. See you tonight?
>
> Love,
>
> Marc

2

> Dear Victoria,
>
> I'm sorry you weren't well last week. Are you better now? Hope to see you tomorrow!
>
> Best wishes,
>
> Simone

3

> Dear Ms. Braun,
>
> I apologize for the delay in this reply. I attach the information about our prices.
>
> Best regards,
>
> Andres Pires

3 Writing skill expressions in emails

a Look at the emails. Complete the chart with expressions for starting and ending emails.

Starting an email	Ending an email
Dear …	All the best
_____	_____
	_____

b Work in pairs. Which expressions are best for: friends and family (F); work or business emails (W)?

c Complete the emails with appropriate expressions from Exercise 3a.

> 1 _____ Mr. Bruni,
>
> I'm very sorry I wasn't in the office yesterday. I hope to see you on your next visit.
>
> 2 _____ ,
>
> Carlos Morales

> 3 _____ Fran,
>
> I was sick on Saturday. I'm sorry I wasn't at your party. Was it fun? I hope so.
>
> 4 _____ ,
>
> Jack

4 Write two emails. Check your expressions.

1 You missed a meeting because your train was late. Apologize to your boss.
2 Your friend was in the hospital last weekend. Express sympathy.

5 Exchange emails with two classmates. Write replies to each other.

10f The space race

The first American
in space

Before you watch

1 Work in pairs. What do you know about the space race? Answer these questions.

1 The space race was between _____.
   a the Soviet Union and the US
   b Germany and the Soviet Union
   c the US and China

2 When did the space race start?
   a the 1930s
   b the 1950s
   c the 1970s

3 Who was the first person to walk on the moon?
   a Buzz Aldrin
   b Neil Armstrong
   c Michael Collins

2 Key vocabulary

a Read the sentences. Match the **bold** words (1–4) with the pictures (a–d).

1 Sputnik was a Soviet **satellite**.
2 **Earth** is a big, blue planet.
3 The **moon** was big and bright last night.
4 Neil Armstrong and Buzz Aldrin were **astronauts**.

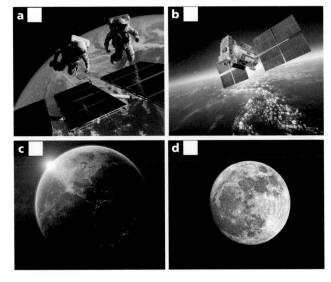

b ▶ 154 Listen and repeat the **bold** words.

While you watch

3 ◖▮ 10 Watch the video. Check your answers in Exercise 1.

4 ◖▮ 10 Watch the video again. Write the years.

1 In 19___, the Soviet Union sent Sputnik to space.
2 In 19___, the Russians sent the first man into space.
3 In 19___, John Glenn flew around Earth three times.
4 In 19___, there was a fire on Apollo 1.
5 In 19___, Neil Armstrong walked on the moon.

5 ◖▮ 10 Work in pairs. What do you remember? Watch the video and check your answers.

1 Who was the US president in 1962?
2 Who was the first man in space?
3 Who was Alan Shepard?
4 What were *Challenger* and *Columbia*?

After you watch

6 Complete the sentences with *was, wasn't, were,* or *weren't*.

1 Sputnik _____ part of the United States' space program.
2 The first man in space _____ Alan Shepard.
3 There _____ a fire on Apollo 1.
4 The first men on the moon _____ Russian.
5 Neil Armstrong and Buzz Aldrin _____ on Apollo 11.

7 Work in groups. Write five important events in the last ten years. Ask and answer questions about the events.

- What happened?
- When was it?
- Where were you?
- Why was the event important?

UNIT 10 REVIEW AND MEMORY BOOSTER

Grammar

1 Complete the article with *was* or *were*.

Sam Sunderland [1] _____ the winner of the 2017 Dakar Rally. He [2] _____ the winner of the motorcycle group, and the first British racer to win. Sam [3] _____ born in 1989. His first win in a motorcycle race [4] _____ in 2010. The winners of the car group in 2017 [5] _____ Stéphane Peterhansel and Jean-Paul Cottret from France. They [6] _____ also winners in 2016.

2 Work in pairs. Put the words in order to make questions.

1 was / the / who / Dakar Rally / first British winner / of the / ?
2 Sam Sunderland / when / born / was / ?
3 the winners / who / in 2017 / of the car group / were / ?

3 ▶▶ MB Work in pairs. Take turns.
Student A: Ask the questions in Exercise 2.
Student B: Answer the questions.

4 ▶▶ MB Work in pairs. How many famous people can you name who:

1 lived in your city?   2 died last year?

I CAN	
talk about the past (*was/were*)	
use *lived* and *died* correctly (simple past)	

Vocabulary

5 Complete the dates in the sentences with *in* or *on*.

1 I was born _____ June 3rd.
2 My sister was born _____ 1987.
3 My baby was born _____ a Friday.
4 My brother was born _____ June, 1995.

6 Circle the correct option.

1 My sister is always *funny / famous*.
2 When I was a child, I wasn't *good / interesting* at math.
3 That band is *famous / nice* here.

7 ▶▶ MB Work in pairs. When were you last:

at home	in traffic	on a train
busy	not well	on the phone

I CAN	
say dates	
describe people (adjectives)	
talk about activities	

Real life

8 Put the conversation in order.

_1_   Hello, Carolyn.
___   The boss was looking for you.
___   I was at home. Why?
___   Yes, thanks.
___   Oh! I'm sorry. I was sick.
___   Hi. Where were you this morning?
___   That's OK. Are you better now?

9 Work in pairs. Practice the conversation in Exercise 8.

I CAN	
make and accept apologies	

Unit 11 True stories

1 Work in pairs. Look at the photo. Which do you think is the best caption for the photo?

  a A man in Timbuktu reads the newspaper.
  b A man in Timbuktu reads old documents.
  c A man in Timbuktu writes a letter to his son.

2 ▶ 155 Listen and check your answer from Exercise 1.

3 ▶ 155 Listen again and complete the sentences.

  1 Timbuktu was a center of learning for _____ of years.
  2 Many of the books and documents were in libraries and family _____ .
  3 Some books are _____ hundred years old.

4 Do you have any old books? Tell the class.

11a Ötzi the Iceman

Reading

1 Read *Ötzi the Iceman*. Work in pairs. Answer the questions.

1 Who found Ötzi?
2 Where was the body?
3 What was Ötzi carrying?
4 What questions did investigators have?

2 Read the article again. Find the past forms of the verbs (1–6) in the article. Write the past forms next to the base forms.

1	be	*was/were*
2	come	_____
3	go	_____
4	have	_____
5	see	_____
6	take	_____

Grammar irregular simple past verbs

▶ **IRREGULAR SIMPLE PAST VERBS**

I/You He/She/It We/You/They	**went** *for a walk.* **saw** *a body.*

Now look at page 178.

3 Look at the grammar box. Then look at this sentence. Circle the correct option.

Irregular simple past verbs *end / don't end* with *-ed*.

4 Complete the sentences with these irregular simple past verbs.

had	saw	took	went

1 Last summer, we _____ to Italy.
2 We _____ some beautiful buildings.
3 We _____ lots of photos.
4 We _____ a great time.

▶ 156

Ötzi the Iceman

In September, 1991, two German tourists were on vacation in the Austrian Alps.

They went for a walk and they saw a body in the ice. The body was very old—it wasn't the body of a climber. There was a knife and some arrows with the body. The police came and they took the body to the University of Innsbruck in Austria.

The police had many questions about the body. Was it a man or a woman? Where was he or she from? How old was the body? But this wasn't a police investigation. It was a scientific investigation.

Listening

5 ▶ 157 Listen to more information about the investigation. Complete the sentences.

1 Ötzi lived about _____ years ago.
2 Ötzi was about _____ years old when he died.

6 ▶ 157 Listen again. Match the two parts of the sentences.

1 The scientists at the University of Innsbruck started ___
2 They called him Ötzi because ___
3 The scientists finished ___

a the body was in the Ötztal mountains.
b their investigation.
c their report about Ötzi.

The Iceman at the South Tyrol Museum of Archaeology in Bolzano, Italy

The Iceman's knife

The Iceman's arrows

7 <u>Underline</u> five regular simple past verbs in Exercises 5 and 6. What are the base forms of these verbs?

_____

8 Complete the sentences. Use the simple past form of the verb.

1 My friend _____*walked*_____ (walk) across the Alps in 2016.
2 I _____ (start) my course last year.
3 Our vacation _____ (end) last Sunday.
4 We _____ (watch) a great movie last week.
5 My mother _____ (be) on a plane with Meryl Streep.

9 Pronunciation *-ed* **regular simple past verbs**

a ▶ 158 Listen to the base and simple past forms of these verbs. Check (✓) the verbs that take on an extra syllable.

☐ call   called
☐ finish   finished
☐ kill   killed
☐ end   ended
☐ start   started

b ▶ 159 Listen and repeat the regular simple past sentences from Exercise 8.

Speaking my Life

10 Tell your partner true and false sentences about your family. Use simple past verbs. Can your partner guess the false sentences?

My parents walked to the South Pole in 2012.

I think that's false!

11 Read the article and track 157 of the audioscript on page 188. Work in pairs. Tell the story of Ötzi with these verbs. Take turns with each sentence.

1 went   5 started
2 saw   6 called
3 came   7 finished
4 took   8 killed

11b Life stories

Vocabulary life events

1 Complete the paragraph with the life events in the box.

lived	studied
met my husband	was born
started work	went to school

I ¹_____ in Japan in 1987. I grew up in a village with my family. We ²_____ in a small house. My sister and I ³_____ in our village. When I was eighteen, I went to California and ⁴_____ mathematics at college. I ⁵_____ when I was twenty-three. My first job was in an office. I ⁶_____ at work.

2 Write true sentences about you with the life events in Exercise 1.

3 Work in pairs. Read your sentences to your partner. What do you have in common?

4 Work in pairs. Read about Caroline Gerdes. Answer the questions.

1 Where was she born?
2 What does she write about?

Caroline Gerdes is a journalist. She was born in New Orleans, and she studied there, too. She writes about the "life story" of her city. She talks to people about their lives and their history. She writes about the life and the culture of New Orleans—Mardi Gras, the story of jazz music, and other things.

Listening

5 ▶ 160 Listen to an interview with Dinah, also from New Orleans. Check (✓) the life events from Exercise 1 that you hear.

☐ was born   ☐ studied at college
☐ lived   ☐ started work
☐ went to school   ☐ met her husband

Mardi Gras in New Orleans

6 ▶ 160 Listen to the interview again. Put the questions in order (1–4).

___ Did you study art in college?
___ Did you live there when you were a child?
___ Why did you decide to be a musician?
___ What did you want to be when you were a child?

7 Work in pairs. Test your memory. What were Dinah's answers to the questions in Exercise 6?

Grammar simple past negative and question forms

▶ **SIMPLE PAST NEGATIVE and QUESTION FORMS**

I/You He/She/It We/You/They	didn't	study art.
Did	I/you he/she/it we/you/they	live there?
Yes, No,	I/you he/she/it we/you/they	did. didn't.

Now look at page 178.

8 Look at the grammar box. Then look at these sentences. Circle the correct option.

1 We use the *base / simple past* form of the verb after *did* in questions.
2 We use the *base / simple past* form of the verb after *didn't*.

9 Work in pairs. Put the words in order to make a question or a negative sentence.

1 didn't / in school / English / study / I / .
   I didn't study English in school.
2 go / college / you / did / to / ?
3 at work / meet / didn't / we / .
4 history / study / didn't / Joseph / .
5 Brazil / live / in / they / did / ?
6 start / Asha / work / did / last year / ?

10 ▶ 161 Complete the questions with *Did you* and these verbs. Then listen and check.

take	live	meet	start	study

1 _Did you study_ English in school?
2 _____ your best friend at school?
3 _____ in a big city when you were young?
4 _____ work this year?
5 _____ a vacation last year?

11 Pronunciation *did you ...?*

a ▶ 161 Listen and repeat the questions from Exercise 10.

b Work in pairs. Ask and answer the questions in Exercise 10.

> Did you study English in school?

> Yes, I did.

> No, I didn't.

Speaking myLife

12 Work in pairs. Write questions about last week or last year.

1 visit a museum
   Did you visit a museum last year?
2 take a vacation

3 pass your English exam

4 go to a concert

13 Who did the things in Exercise 12? Work as a class. Walk around. Ask and answer questions, and write sentences.

> Did you visit a museum last year?

> Yes, I did. I went with two friends.

Lidia visited a museum last year.

11c A problem in Madagascar

Reading

1 Work in pairs. Look at the photos. Which things do you think these adjectives describe?

beautiful	dangerous	fantastic
interesting	unusual	

2 Work in pairs. Read the article and answer the questions.

1 Where did Neil Shea go?
2 Who did he go with?
3 Why did he go to the *tsingy*?
4 What did they see?

3 Read the last paragraph of the article again. Put the events in order (1–4).

____ Neil Shea went to the hospital.
____ The nurse asked him a question.
____ Neil Shea fell and cut his leg.
____ The nurse cleaned his leg.

Critical thinking the writer's purpose

4 Work in pairs. Read the passage again. Why do you think the author wrote this article (e.g., to teach people)? Is there more than one reason? Who is the article for?

Grammar simple past *Wh-* questions

► **SIMPLE PAST *WH-* QUESTIONS**

What Where When Why Who	did	I/you/he/she/it we/you/they	do? go? get there? go? meet?

Now look at page 178.

5 Look at the grammar box. Then look at the questions in Exercise 2. <u>Underline</u> the question words.

6 Complete the questions about Neil Shea with the correct *Wh-* word.

Why	What	~~When~~	Who

1 _When_ did he go to Madagascar?
2 _____ did he go to the hospital?
3 _____ did he talk to in the the hospital?
4 _____ did she say?

7 Work in pairs. Ask and answer the questions in Exercise 6.

8 Word focus *get*

a Look at the sentence from the article. Circle the sentence (1–4) with the same meaning of *get*.

We got there after five days.

1 Did you get my message?
2 I got a ticket for the plane to Cairo.
3 Can you get a bus from the airport?
4 I got home on Friday.

b What does *got* mean in each sentence? Use these words.

received	arrived	bought	took

1 I *got* these clothes at the shopping mall.
_____

2 We missed the train, so we *got* a taxi.
_____

3 He *got* there at nine o'clock. _____

4 We *got* an email from our friends.
_____

Speaking *my*Life

9 Work in pairs. Ask and answer *Wh-* questions about a day from last week. Find one thing you both did.

> What did you have for breakfast?

> I had toast and coffee.

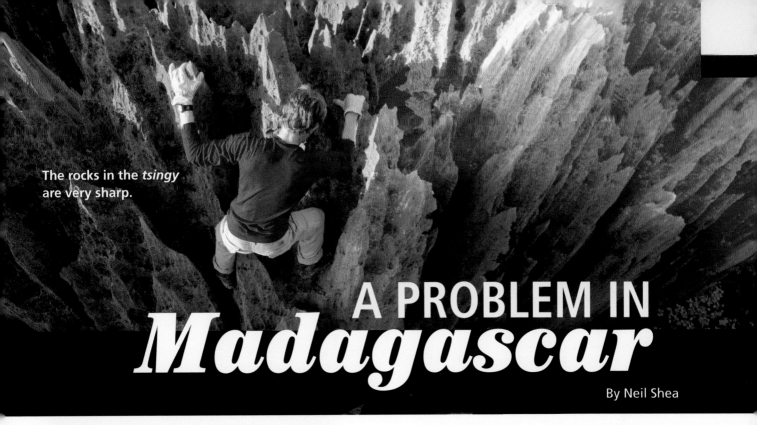

The rocks in the *tsingy* are very sharp.

A PROBLEM IN
Madagascar

By Neil Shea

▶ 162

Madagascar is a fantastic place. About ninety percent of the animals and plants there live only in Madagascar. There are some very unusual animals and plants in Madagascar's Tsingy de Bemaraha National Park, but it's a dangerous place. The rocks—the *tsingy*—in the park are very sharp. The word *tsingy* means "you can't walk here" in the Malagasy language.

I went to Madagascar in March. It was the end of the rainy season. I was with a scientist and a photographer. We wanted to find some new animals and plants. We traveled to the park with our guide. We got there after five days.

We walked through the *tsingy*. The rocks cut our clothes and our shoes. It was very dangerous, but we saw hundreds of animals and plants. We saw beautiful birds and unusual white lemurs with red eyes. They didn't have any problems on the *tsingy* rocks!

Then, one afternoon, I fell on a rock. I cut my leg. The cut was very bad and very dirty. We were a long way from a town. After two days, I got to a hospital. The nurse cleaned my leg. She asked me a question. "Why did you go to the *tsingy*? Madagascans don't go to the *tsingy* because it's dangerous." It's true. The *tsingy* is dangerous, but it's also amazing.

Plants growing in the tsingy

This lemur lives only in Madagascar

Did you have a good time?

Real life talking about the past

1 Work in pairs. Look at the photo. What can you see?

2 ▶163 Listen to three conversations. Write the number of the conversation (1–3).

The people …
a had a meal. ___
b were in Sydney. ___
c didn't take a vacation. ___

3 ▶163 Listen again and answer the questions for each conversation (1–3).

1 Did they go swimming? _____
2 Did they stay home? _____
3 Did they pay for the meal? _____

4 Pronunciation *didn't*

a ▶164 Listen to three sentences from the conversations. Notice how the *t* in *didn't* isn't stressed.

b ▶164 Listen and repeat the sentences.

Vocabulary time expressions

5 ▶163 Listen to the three conversations again. Check (✓) the expressions you hear.

☐ on Friday   ☐ last weekend
☐ last night   ☐ yesterday
☐ last week   ☐ last year

6 Work in pairs. Say one thing you did using each of the time expressions in Exercise 5.

> *I had a nice meal on Friday.*

▶ TALKING ABOUT THE PAST

Did you have a good vacation last year?
Did you have a good time in Sydney last week?
Did you have a nice meal last night?
Why not?
There was a shark in the water!
We didn't go swimming.
It was delicious.

7 Work in pairs. Look at track 163 of the audioscript on page 189. Practice the conversations.

8 Work in pairs. Choose an event and a time expression. Ask and answer questions about the event. Say something you didn't do, and give a reason.

a day at the beach	last month
a vacation	last night
a meal	last week
a party	on Saturday
a trip	yesterday

> *Hi. Did you have a good day at the beach yesterday?*

> *Yes, I did. But I didn't go in the water.*

> *Why not?*

> *It was very cold!*

11e Childhood memories

Writing a life story

1 Work in pairs. Do you like to read the life stories of famous people? Who?

2 Read about Tyler. Which paragraphs (A–C) give information about these things?

1 toys ___ 2 family ___ 3 school ___

3 Work in pairs. Read about Tyler again and answer the questions.

1 When was Tyler born?
2 Who did he live with?
3 What was his favorite toy?
4 Did he like school?

4 Writing skill *when*

a Complete the sentence from the text.

When I was seven, _____

_____

b <u>Underline</u> three more sentences with *When* in the text.

c Work in pairs. Combine the sentences using *When*. Don't forget the comma.

1 My parents were young. They lived in India.
2 I was a child. I had lots of toys.
3 I was three years old. My sister was born.

5 Make notes about your childhood. Answer the questions from Exercise 3, but about yourself.

6 Use your notes to write three paragraphs about your childhood memories. Include a sentence with *When*.

7 Check your spelling, punctuation, and verbs.

8 Work in pairs. Exchange paragraphs. Ask your partner questions about his or her childhood.

MY CHILDHOOD MEMORIES
Tyler

A I was born in Kansas City on July 15th, 1995. When I was a child, I lived with my brother, my parents, and my grandfather. My grandfather was funny and interesting. He died in 2010.

B When I was seven, my favorite toy was a red helicopter. I got it from my grandfather. When my friends saw my helicopter, they wanted it.

C I went to school with my brother every day. We were in the same class because we're twins. I didn't like school very much. When I was sixteen, I left school and I started my first job the next day. That was the end of my childhood.

11f True stories?

Fireworks in the
night sky

Before you watch

1 Work in pairs. Look at the photo and the caption on page 100. What is happening?

2 Key vocabulary

a Read the sentences. Match the **bold** words (1–4) with the pictures (a–d).

1 An **ambulance** took my brother to hospital.
2 We can carry water in a **bucket**.
3 We have new **curtains** in the living room.
4 I passed my English **test**!

b ▶ **165** Listen and repeat the **bold** words.

3 Work in pairs. What are the base forms of these simple past verbs?

1 ate	6 knew	11 stopped
2 cut	7 lit	12 threw
3 fell	8 opened	13 took
4 had	9 said	14 went
5 hid	10 started	15 passed

While you watch

4 ▮◀ **11.1** Watch Part 1 of the video. Match the groups of verbs with the stories (1–3)

_____ started, had, opened, lit, threw
_____ had, hid, knew, say
_____ went, fell, cut, stopped, took, ate

5 ▮◀ **11.1** Watch Part 1 of the video again. We don't hear the interviewer's questions. Write the number of the story (1–3) next to the question.

a Did the teacher find you? _____
b What happened? What did you do? _____
c How long was the ride? _____

6 ▮◀ **11.2** Work in pairs. Do you think the stories are true or false? Watch Part 2 of the video and check.

After you watch

7 Work in pairs. What can you remember?

1 Was the person in the closet a boy or a girl?

_____

2 How did the person in story 2 cut her leg?

_____

3 What month was it in story 3?

_____

8 Work in pairs. Choose one of the stories. Try to tell the story.

> *When Amanda was about ten or eleven, she had a math test.*

> *She was very bad at math, so she ...*

UNIT 11 REVIEW AND MEMORY BOOSTER

Grammar

1 Complete the blog post with the simple past forms of the verbs.

Last month, I was with a group of people on a boat. We ¹ _____ (be) in Alaska. Justin Hofman, a scuba diver, ² _____ (be) in the water. He ³ _____ (have) a camera. He ⁴ _____ (take) pictures and ⁵ _____ (send) them to us up on the boat. There was a video and an audio connection, too. Justin ⁶ _____ (talk) about the animals and plants he ⁷ _____ (see), and we ⁸ _____ (ask) him questions. It was a great experience!

Posted by Carly

2 Work in pairs. Read Carly's answers. Write the questions.

1 No, I didn't go into the water.
2 Yes, I had a great time.
3 I went with my friends.

3 >> MB Work in pairs. You were on the boat in the photo. Ask and answer questions with these words.

1 Where / go?   3 What / see?
2 When / arrive?   4 Why / go?

I CAN	
talk about the past (regular and irregular simple past verbs)	
ask and answer questions about the past (question words)	

Vocabulary

4 Read about David's day. Complete the sentences with seven of these verbs.

bought	cleaned	cut	drove	fell
found	met	paid	sent	took

Yesterday, I ¹ _____ lunch for my friend. I ² _____ twenty dollars outside my house. I ³ _____ a text to my friend Alex. We ⁴ _____ at my house and we ⁵ _____ to a cafe together. I ⁶ _____ for lunch with the twenty dollars. Alex ⁷ _____ a photo of our meal.

5 >> MB Work in pairs. Write true sentences about you. Use the verbs from Exercise 4 and these time expressions:

Last night/weekend/week/month/year

Read your sentences to each other. Did you do the same things?

I CAN	
say when people did things	

Real life

6 Read the conversation between two colleagues. Circle the best option.

A: Did you have ¹ *a good day at the beach / a nice meal / a good vacation* last night?
B: No, I didn't.
A: Oh? Why not?
B: The food was delicious, but my friend ² *missed the plane / saw a shark in the water / cut her hand with her knife*!

7 Work in pairs. Practice the conversation in Exercise 6.

I CAN	
give reasons for events in the past	

Unit 12 The weekend

Friends having lunch in Riyadh, Saudi Arabia

FEATURES

1 Work in pairs. Look at the photo of friends on their day off work. What are your days off?

2 Look at these weekend activities. Do people do these at home (H), outside (O), or both (B)?

___ cook a meal	___ meet friends
___ meet family	___ play soccer
___ go shopping	___ play video games
___ go out for a meal	___ watch a concert

3 ▶ 166 Listen to three friends. Circle the activities in Exercise 2 that they talk about.

4 Work in pairs. How often do you do the weekend activities in Exercise 2? Is your weekend similar or different to your partner's?

I often play video games on weekends.

Me too.

12a At home

Vocabulary rooms in a house

1 Match the things (1–5) with the rooms.

bathroom	bedroom	dining room
~~kitchen~~	living room	

1 a stove, a fridge ___kitchen___
2 a chair, a table _____
3 an armchair, a couch _____
4 a bed, a wardrobe _____
5 a bathtub, a shower,
   a toilet _____

2 ▶ 167 Listen and check your answers from Exercise 1.

3 ▶ 168 Listen and repeat the words for the rooms.

4 Work in pairs. Tell your partner one thing about each room in your home.

> *We don't have a dining room. We eat in the kitchen.*

> *My kitchen is very small.*

Listening

5 Work in pairs. Look at the photos (1–5) of a family at home in Indonesia. Which rooms from Exercise 1 can you see?

6 ▶ 169 Match the sentences (a–e) with the photos (1–5). Listen and check.

a They're washing their motorcycles.
b She's making lunch.
c He's playing a video game with his son.
d He's bathing his daughter.
e They're drinking coffee.

7 ▶ 169 Listen again. Say who the sentences in Exercise 6 are about.

> *She's making lunch.*   *Ayu's mother*

HOME LIFE
PHOTO PROJECT

This is Ayu's home and family in Sumatra, Indonesia. It's a Saturday morning.

1

3

4

Grammar present continuous

Now look at page 180.

▶ PRESENT CONTINUOUS		
I	am (not)	talking.
You/We/You/They	are (not)	cooking.
He/She/It	is (not)	making lunch.

8 Look at the grammar box. Then look at the sentences in Exercise 6. Which auxiliary verb do we use to make the present continuous? _____

9 Complete the sentences about the photos.

1 Ayu's mother _is cooking_ . (cook)
2 Amir and his daughter _____ . (smile)
3 Ayu's father and his friend _____ (drink) coffee.
4 Amir's brother _____ (play) a video game with his son.
5 Ayu's brother _____ (wear) an orange T-shirt.

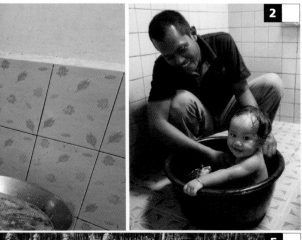

10 Work in pairs. Look at the photos again and write true sentences. Use the negative form.

1 Ayu's mother / eat
   Ayu's mother isn't eating.
2 Amir / smile at the camera
3 Ayu's father and his friend / stand
4 Amir's brother / watch TV
5 Ayu's brother / wash a car

▶ PRESENT CONTINUOUS QUESTIONS and SHORT ANSWERS			
(What)	Am	I	reading? doing?
	Are	you/we/you/they	
	Is	he/she/it	
Yes, I am. No, I'm not. Yes, you/we/you/they are. No, you/we/you/they aren't. Yes, she/he/it is. No, she/he/it isn't.			

Now look at page 180.

11 Look at the grammar box. Circle the correct question form (a–c).

a Are you play?
b He is playing?
c Are they playing?

12 Work in pairs. Write questions about the photos. Ask and answer the questions.

Photo 1: she / cook?
Photo 2: what / the baby / look at?
Photo 3: they / eat?
Photo 4: what / they / do?
Photo 5: what / they / wash?

13 Work in pairs. Turn to page 157.

Speaking myLife

14 Work in groups. Show some of your photos. Ask and answer questions.

Who's that? What's he doing?	That's my cousin. He's singing.

12b Next weekend

Reading

1 Look at the information about three events. Complete the chart.

	What?	Where?	When?
a		a shop	
b	a talk		
c			

2 Read the messages between two friends, Alex and Lauren. Which event (a–c) in Exercise 1 are they talking about? ___

Monday

A: What are you doing next weekend? Do you want to meet on Saturday?

L: Sorry, I can't. I'm going for a walk with my sister on Saturday.

A: How about Sunday? I'm going to a concert in the evening at City Hall.

L: Sure. Send me the details.

Grammar present continuous for the future

▶ **PRESENT CONTINUOUS FOR THE FUTURE**

*What are you doing **next weekend**?*
*I'm going for a walk with my sister **on Saturday**.*
*I'm going to a concert **in the evening**.*

Now look at page 180.

3 Look at the grammar box. Are the sentences about now (N) or a time in the future (F)? ___

4 ▶ 170 Work in pairs. Use the present continuous tense. Complete the conversation about the talk by Helen Smith in Exercise 1. Then listen and check.

A: What / you / do / next weekend?
B: I'm not sure. My brother / come over / tomorrow.
A: he / stay the weekend?
B: Yes, he is. We / go out / for dinner / Saturday evening.
A: Helen Smith / give a talk / Sunday afternoon. Do you want to come?
B: Yes, that's a great idea.

5 Work in pairs. Practice the conversation in Exercise 4.

6 Pronunciation *going* and *doing*

a ▶171 Listen to four sentences. Pay attention to the /w/ sound in *going* and *doing*.

b ▶172 Listen again and repeat the sentences.

7 Work in pairs. Look at the information about people's activities for next weekend. Write true sentences with these words. Use affirmative and negative forms.

1 Aisha / shopping / Sunday morning
Aisha isn't going shopping on Sunday morning.
2 Aisha / a cake / Saturday afternoon
3 Aisha / tennis / Sunday afternoon
4 Bernardo / friends / Saturday afternoon
5 Bernardo / TV / Sunday afternoon
6 Che and Dan / walk / Saturday morning
7 Che and Dan / soccer / Sunday morning
8 Che and Dan / Che's parents / Sunday morning

		Saturday	Sunday
Aisha	a.m.	go shopping	play tennis
	p.m.	make a cake	
Bernardo	a.m.	meet friends	
	p.m.		watch TV
Che and Dan	a.m.	go for a walk	play soccer
	p.m.		visit Che's parents

Speaking *my* Life

8 Make plans for next weekend. Write activities for these times.

Saturday

MORNING	
AFTERNOON	
EVENING	

Sunday

MORNING	
AFTERNOON	
EVENING	

9 Work in pairs. Take turns to invite your partner to do activities with you.

Do you want to go shopping on Saturday morning?

Sorry, I'm playing soccer. What about the afternoon?

Saturday afternoon in a cafe in Paris

12c A different kind of weekend

Reading

1 Work in pairs. Look at the photos and answer the questions.

1 What do you think the people are doing?
2 Do you think there is anything unusual about them?

2 Read *A different kind of weekend* and check your answers for Exercise 1.

Critical thinking finding main ideas

3 Work in pairs. Circle the main idea of the article.

a Tornadoes damage homes in Kansas.
b We can help people in our free time.
c Joel Connor is an unusual person.

Underline sentences in the article that show the main idea.

Grammar prepositions of place

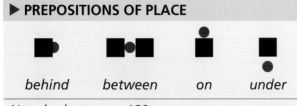

▶ **PREPOSITIONS OF PLACE**

behind   between   on   under

Now look at page 180.

4 Look at the grammar box. Read the sentences and look at the photos. Write S (small photo) or L (large photo).

1 There are four people on the roof. _L_
2 The house is behind the woman in the green top. ___
3 The green board is between two blue boards. ___
4 The blue board is under the woman's hand. ___

Grammar tense review

▶ **TENSE REVIEW**

1 *Joel Connor works in an office in Kansas.*
2 *The community started a project.*
3 *Joel is working with Jill and Scott Eller.*
4 *Next weekend, Joel is moving to a different project.*

5 Work in pairs. Look at the grammar box. Underline the verbs in the sentences. Do they describe the past, present, or future?

6 Complete the answers with the correct forms of the verbs.

1 Sam _____ (go) to work every day.
2 Last year, Ian _____ (move) to a new house.
3 Next week, we _____ (help) our friend fix his car.

7 Match the questions (1–3) with the answers (a–c). Then write P (past), PR (present), or F (future) next to the answers.
1 What are you doing? ___
2 What did you do last weekend? ___
3 What are you doing over the weekend? ___

a I'm going to a concert on Saturday. ___
b I visited my cousin in Boston. ___
c I'm making lunch. ___

Speaking myLife

8 Work in groups. Plan a special weekend for a person you all know. Then tell the class.

Next weekend, we are taking Esther shopping. After that, ...

A different kind of weekend

▶ 172

Joel Connor works in an office in Kansas. His job is a typical nine-to-five, Monday-to-Friday job. On weekends, he does something different. He helps people build houses for free. Every weekend, there's a new project. This weekend, Joel is helping Jill and Scott Eller. You can see him in the photo. He's moving a large blue board. All of the people in the photo are "weekend builders."

These "weekend builders" are from the small town of Greensburg in Kansas. A year ago, a tornado hit their town. After the tornado, the community started a project to build new homes. The goal is to build a total of thirty homes.

Joel says, "I heard about the tornado and the new project. I knew some people in Greensburg. I wanted to help." Joel is working with Jill and Scott Eller to build their dream house. They're making the house tornado-resistant—that's why it has an unusual shape.

The Ellers' house is now almost ready. Next weekend, Joel is moving to a different project. Why does he do this on weekends? "I have time, I can help people, I make friends, and it's fun! So why not?"

12d Would you like to come?

Vocabulary times and places

1 Look at the expressions for times and places. <u>Underline</u> the prepositions.

1 **next** week / month / year / Friday / _____

2 **tomorrow** morning / night / _____

3 **on** the table / _____
4 **on Tuesday** morning / afternoon / _____

5 **in the** morning / afternoon / _____
6 **in** town / _____
7 **at** our house / _____
8 **at** eight o'clock / _____

2 Work in pairs. Add one more time or place to each expression in Exercise 1.

Real life offers and invitations

3 ▶173 Listen to a conversation between Brad, Samira, and Kris.

1 Who's moving house? _____
2 When's he/she moving? _____
3 What's happening in the old house on Sunday? _____

4 ▶173 Listen to the conversation again. Look at the expressions below. Listen for the expressions in the conversation.

> **OFFERS AND INVITATIONS**

Would you like a drink?
Would you like to come?
Do you want to have lunch?
I'd like to come.
I'd like a cup of tea.
Sorry, I can't make it.
Yes, please.

---

5 Pronunciation *would you …?*

a ▶174 Listen to four *would you like* questions. Pay attention to the /dʒ/ sound in *would you*.

b ▶174 Listen again and repeat the questions.

c Work in pairs. Make offers and invitations with *would you like*.

to watch a movie	a cup of coffee
to play soccer	a seat
to join us for lunch	a glass of water

6 Work in new pairs. Take turns to make offers for each situation. How many offers can you make?

Your partner is …

- cold
- hungry
- thirsty
- tired

Would you like my jacket?

No, thanks.

Would you like a hat?

12e Thank you!

Writing a thank you note

1 Work in pairs. Look at the photo. What's the problem?

2 Read the note. A part of the note (...) is missing. Read the pairs of sentences (a–c). Circle the pair that completes the note.

> Dear Lili,
>
> Thank you for a fantastic weekend! We had a great time. On the way home, something happened. ... We're using Dad's car this week—he's taking the train to work. Speak to you soon.
>
> Best wishes,
>
> Bibia and Mark

a Our plane was late! So we stayed in a hotel for the night.

b We went on the wrong road! We got home at midnight!

c We had a problem with the car! So I called my parents to help us.

3 Writing skill spelling: verb endings

a Work in pairs. <u>Underline</u> the two verbs below in the note. Write their base forms. What's the spelling change?

1 using _____   2 taking _____

b Complete the chart.

	Present continuous	Simple present (*he/she/it*)	Simple past
come	_____	_____	_____
do	_____	_____	_____
drive	_____	_____	drove
make	_____	_____	made
see	_____	_____	_____
study	_____	_____	_____
swim	_____	_____	swam

4 Choose one of these sentences. Write a thank you note to a friend. Include one of the adjectives.

- A friend sent you some photos.
- You had a meal at a friend's house.
- A friend gave you some books.
- You stayed with a friend for the weekend.

amazing	beautiful	fantastic
great	interesting	nice

5 Check your note. Check the simple past verbs.

6 Work in pairs. Exchange notes. Ask a follow-up question about your partner's note.

12f A day in the life of a lighthouse keeper

The lighthouse at Cabo
Polonio in Uruguay

Before you watch

1 Work in pairs. Look at the photo on page 150. Where do we usually see lighthouses?

2 Complete the paragraph about Cabo Polonio with these words.

> coast   lighthouse   people   road

Cabo Polonio is a small village on the east ¹ _____ of Uruguay. It's not easy to get to Cabo Polonio. The main ² _____ is seven kilometers away. There are about 95 ³ _____ in the village and there is a tall ⁴ _____ . It was built in 1881.

3 Key vocabulary

a Read the sentences. Match the **bold** words (1–3) with the pictures (a–c).

1 We often eat **stew** in winter.
2 *Mate* is a popular South American drink.
3 I use **tools** a lot in my job.

 **a**

 **b**

 **c**

b ▶ 175 Listen and repeat the **bold** words.

4 Work in pairs. The person who works in a lighthouse is called a lighthouse keeper. What do you think he or she does?

While you watch

5 ◀ 12 Watch the video. Complete the activities with these words.

> clothes   a machine   outside

___ cleaning _____ ___
___ cleaning stairs
___ cutting meat
___ making *mate*
_1_ repairing things
___ sitting _____
___ washing _____

6 ◀ 12 Watch the video again. Number the activities in Exercise 5 in order (1–7).

After you watch

7 Work in pairs. Write the commentary for the video. Follow these steps:

1 Describe the weather.
   It's a cloudy day.
2 Introduce the lighthouse keeper. Give him a name.
3 Describe the activities from Exercise 5 and add your own ideas.
4 Try reading your commentary while the video plays. Take turns.

8 Work in pairs. What would you like to ask the lighthouse keeper? Write three questions.

> *When did you become a lighthouse keeper?*

> *Do you like your job?*

9 Work in pairs. Imagine you are the lighthouse keeper. Answer your questions from Exercise 8. Take turns.

UNIT 12 REVIEW AND MEMORY BOOSTER

Grammar

1 Work in pairs. Look at the photo of a bus stop in Santiago, Chile. Match the words (1–4) with the people (a–d). Then write sentences with the present continuous.

1 make / a phone call
2 wear / a brown jacket
3 carry / some books
4 talk / to her friend

2 Complete the paragraph about the photo with the present continuous.

It's Friday evening in Santiago. People
[1] _____ (stand) at a bus stop. There's a bus. Its doors [2] _____ (open), but the people [3] _____ (not get) on the bus. They [4] _____ (wait) for different buses.
Some of them [5] _____ (go) home. They [6] _____ (think) about the weekend. Some [7] _____ (not go) home. They [8] _____ (take) the bus to work.

3 ▶▶ MB Work in pairs. Ask and answer questions with the present continuous.

1 you / go to the concert / Tuesday?
2 where / you / go / tomorrow?
3 you / meet friends / this weekend?

I CAN

talk about now (present continuous)	☐
talk about the future (present continuous with future time expressions)	☐

Vocabulary

4 ▶▶ MB Work in pairs. Where do people do these things? Ask and answer questions about rooms with these words.

1 make meals   4 watch TV
2 sleep   5 eat
3 take a shower   6 read

5 ▶▶ MB Work in pairs. Tell your partner about the things you usually do on weekends. Do you do similar things?

I CAN

talk about rooms in a house	☐
talk about weekend activities	☐

Real life

6 Match the offers and invitations (1–4) with the responses (a–d).

1 Would you like a drink? ___
2 Are you hungry? Do you want a sandwich? ___
3 Do you want to meet on Sunday? ___
4 Would you like to watch a movie tomorrow? ___

a OK, sure. I'm free on Sunday.
b Sorry, I can't make it tomorrow.
c Yes, please. I'd like a glass of water.
d No, thanks. I ate a burger just now.

7 Work in pairs. Practice the exchanges in Exercise 6. Change the responses.

I CAN

make and respond to offers and invitations	☐

UNIT 2b, Exercise 13, page 25
Student A

1 Look at the photo. You are on vacation in Oman. Look at the sentences (1 5) and choose from the options. Then have a telephone conversation with Student B. Answer his or her questions.

1 I'm in Oman.
2 It's *hot / cold*.
3 I'm *OK / happy*.
4 The beach is *nice / beautiful*.
5 My hotel is *nice / OK*.

2 Your friend (Student B) is on vacation. Prepare questions with these words. Then have a telephone conversation with Student B. Ask the questions.

1 where?
2 cold?
3 OK?
4 city beautiful?
5 hotel nice?

UNIT 4b, Exercise 8, page 49
Student A

1 Look at the information about photo A. Answer your partner's questions.

The Paranel Observatory
- Atacama desert in Chile.
- Open on Saturdays.
- It's big. It's in the James Bond movie *Quantum of Solace.*

2 Look at photo B. Ask your partner the questions in the grammar box on page 49.

UNIT 8b, Exercise 11, page 97

Student A

1 Look at the information. Ask questions about Paulo to complete the chart.

Does Paulo watch videos online?

2 Answer your partner's questions about Eva.

3 Complete the information for "You."

4 Answer your partner's questions.

5 Ask your partner questions and complete the information for "Your partner."

Do you watch videos online?

6 Are you or your partner similar to Paulo or Eva?

	 Paulo	 Eva	You	Your partner
watch videos online?		✓		
go to classes in the evenings?		✓		
drink coffee?		✓		
do homework on weekends?		✗ after school		
have lunch at home?		✗ at work		
meet friends after class?		✗ on Sundays		

UNIT 9b, Exercise 12, page 109

Student A

Ask your partner about the Sun Hotel. Then look at the information about the Mountain Hotel. Answer your partner's questions. Decide which of the three hotels you want to stay in.

	Seaview Hotel	Mountain Hotel	Sun Hotel
free Wi-Fi?	✓	✓	
a parking lot?	✓	✓	
a restaurant?	✓	✗	
rooms with a fridge?	✓	✗	
a swimming pool?	✓	✗	
buses to the city center?	✗	✓	
cost per night	$145	$90	

UNIT 2b, Exercise 13, page 25
Student B

1 Your friend (Student A) is on vacation. Prepare questions with these words. Then have a telephone conversation with Student A. Ask the questions.

1 where?
2 hot?
3 OK?
4 beach beautiful?
5 hotel nice?

2 Look at the photo. You are on vacation in New York. Look at the sentences (1–5) and choose from the options. Then have a telephone conversation with Student A. Answer his or her questions.

1 I'm in New York.
2 It's *hot / cold*.
3 I'm *OK / happy*.
4 The city is *nice / beautiful*.
5 My hotel is *nice / OK*.

UNIT 4b, Exercise 8, page 49
Student B

1 Look at photo A. Ask your partner the questions in the grammar box on page 49.

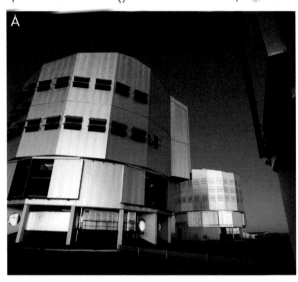

2 Look at the information about photo B. Answer your partner's questions.

The Taj Mahal
- Agra in India.
- Open every day except Fridays.
- It's beautiful. It's a UNESCO World Heritage Site.

UNIT 8b, Exercise 11, page 97

Student B

1 Look at the information. Answer your partner's questions about Paulo.

2 Ask questions about Eva to complete the chart.

> *Does Eva watch videos online?*

3 Complete the information for "You."

4 Ask your partner questions and complete the information for "Your partner."

> *Do you watch videos online?*

5 Answer your partner's questions.

6 Are you or your partner similar to Paulo or Eva?

	 Paulo	 Eva	You	Your partner
watch videos online?	✗ on TV			
go to classes in the evenings?	✓			
drink coffee?	✗ tea			
do homework on weekends?	✓			
have lunch at home?	✗ at school			
meet friends after class?	✓			

UNIT 9b, Exercise 12, page 109

Student B

Look at the information about the Sun Hotel. Answer your partner's questions. Then ask about the Mountain Hotel. Decide which of the three hotels you want to stay in.

	Seaview Hotel	Mountain Hotel	Sun Hotel
free Wi-Fi?	✓		✓
a parking lot?	✓		✓
a restaurant?	✓		✓
rooms with a fridge?	✓		✗
a swimming pool?	✓		✗
buses to the city center?	✗		✓
cost per night	$145		$110

UNIT 6c, Exercise 9, page 74

Student A

Look at the photos and choose an item. Answer your partner's questions. You can answer yes or no. Repeat with two or three more items. Take turns.

Student B

Look at the photos. Ask questions to find out your partner's item. You can ask questions with yes or no answers. Repeat with two or three more items. Take turns.

> *Can you have it for breakfast / lunch / dinner?*

> *Is it a fruit / vegetable / snack?*

> *Is it a food / drink?*

> *Is it red / white / brown?*   *Is it hot / cold?*

 avocado   cereal   cheese

 lemonade   milk   orange juice

 pasta   soup   yogurt

UNIT 12a, Exercise 13, page 143

Student A

Look at the photo of Ayu's family in the living room. Write questions. Then ask and answer the questions with your partner.

1 children / watch TV?
2 man / sit on a chair?
3 people in the kitchen / talk?

Student B

Look at the photo of Ayu's family in the living room. Write questions. Then ask and answer the questions with your partner.

1 boy / lie on the couch?
2 girls / sit on the floor?
3 women on the couch / eat?

GRAMMAR SUMMARY UNIT 1

be: I + am, you + are

| I | am ('m) | Simon. |
| You | are ('re) | Anna. |

Contractions

I'm = I am
You're = You are

I'm Simon.

I'm Anna.

You're Anna.

You're Simon.

▶ Exercises 1 and 2

be: he/she/it + is

He	is ('s)	from São Paulo.
She	is ('s)	Brazilian.
It	is ('s)	in Brazil.

Contractions

He's = He is
She's = She is
It's = It is

He is   She is   It is

▶ Exercises 3 and 4

be: I + am, you + are, he/she/it + is

I	am ('m)	John.
You	are ('re)	a student.
He	is ('s)	Spanish.
She	is ('s)	from Vietnam.
It	is ('s)	in Italy.

▶ Exercises 5 and 6

my, your

I'm Simon. **My** name's Simon.
You're Anna. **Your** name's Anna.

It's my book.

It's your book.

My name's Maya.

Your name's John.

▶ Exercise 7

Exercises

1 Write *I'm* or *You're*.

Hello. _I'm_ Jack.

Hi. _____ Susana.

Hello. _____ your teacher. _____ in my class.

2 Write *I'm* or *You're*.

1 GEORGE: _____ George.
  TERESA: Hi, George.
2 CAROLA: Hi, George.
  GEORGE: Hello! _____ Carola!
3 TERESA: Hello.
  OTTO: Hi! _____ Otto Hampel.

3 Write *He*, *She*, or *It*.

She 's Italian.

_____'s a chair.

_____'s from Egypt.

_____'s an English book.

_____'s American.

_____'s from Mexico.

4 Write sentences with *He's*, *She's*, and *It's*.

1 Jack / from London
  He's from London.
2 George / Canadian
  _____
3 Katya / Russian
  _____
4 Chicago / in the United States
  _____
5 Jessica / from Toronto
  _____
6 Cairo / in Egypt
  _____

5 Write *am*, *are*, and *is*.

1 Hi! I _____ Elena.
2 Paul _____ a doctor.
3 He _____ from Hong Kong.
4 It _____ in China.
5 You _____ American.

6 Put the words in order to make sentences. Use contractions if possible.

1 is / the United States / it / from
  It's from the United States.
2 Mexico / is / Elisabeth / from
  _____
3 Spanish / is / the teacher
  _____
4 is / Brazilian / he
  _____
5 in / New York / am / I
  _____

7 Complete the sentences with *my* and *your*.

1 _____ name's Ludmilla. I'm from Russia.
2 Hello! I'm Tomas. You're my teacher.
  _____ name's Mr. Jones.
3 Hi. I'm Juan. What's _____ name?
4 A: _____ cell phone number is 555 836 736.
  B: Thanks.
5 A: Ben, what's _____ home number?
  B: It's 555 497 268.

GRAMMAR SUMMARY UNIT 2

be: *we/they + are*

We	are ('re)	in Canada.
They	are ('re)	on a beach.
		doctors.

Contractions
We're = We are   *They're = They are*

We're on a beach.

They're doctors.

▶ **Exercises 1 and 2**

be: negative forms

I	**am not ('m not)**	a teacher.
You	**are not (aren't)**	from Italy.
He/She/It	**is not (isn't)**	on a beach.
We/You/They	**are not (aren't)**	from Italy. on a beach.

Contractions
aren't = are not   *isn't = is not*

▶ **Exercise 3**

be: questions and short answers

Questions	
Are you	in a hotel?
Is he/she/it	cold?
Are we/you/they	from California?
Short answers	
Yes, I **am**. / No, I'**m not**.	
Yes, he/she/it **is**. / No, he/she/it **isn't**.	
Yes, we/you/they **are**. / No, we/you/they **aren't**.	

Affirmative form → Question form
  It's cold.   →   **Is it** cold?

  it is   →   *is it*

Short answers
  Yes, I am. ✓   Yes, ~~I'm.~~ ✗
  Yes, he/she/it is. ✓   Yes, ~~he's / she's / it's.~~ ✗
  Yes, we/you/they are. ✓ Yes, ~~we're /you're /~~
                          ~~they're.~~ ✗

▶ **Exercises 4 and 5**

a/an

a book, **a** city
an animal, **an** island

a/an = one thing

a + single noun with consonants: *b, c, d, f*, etc.
an + single noun with vowels: *a, e, i, o, u*

EDUCATION
CONFERENCE
Josh Lees LONDON
10-14 May

a phone   *an ID card*

▶ **Exercise 6**

Plural nouns

book**s**, cit**ies**, beach**es**

Spelling changes
Add *-s*.
  a car   →   *cars*
  airport, door, lake, photo, student, table, etc.
Change *y* to *ies*.
  a country →   *countries*
Add *-es* to nouns that end in *-s*, *-ch*, and *-ss*.
  a bus   →   *buses*
  a car   →   *cars* ✓ ~~a cars~~ ✗

Television   International
Marina
BRUNETTI
VISITOR   12 / 14 / 2018
EDUCATION
CONFERENCE
Josh Lees LONDON
10-14 May

phones   *ID cards*

▶ **Exercise 7**

Exercises

1 Complete the sentences with *We* or *They*.

_____'re in Paris.

_____'re taxis.

_____'re in London.

_____'re Spanish.

2 Complete the sentences.

1 This is Jack. This is Bill. __*They*__ are Canadian.
2 France and Spain _____ in Europe.
3 Bruno and Paola are from Italy. _____ Italian.
4 I'm with my teacher. _____'re in a classroom.
5 I'm from Japan. My friend is from Japan. _____ Japanese.

3 Rewrite the sentences with the verb in the negative form.

1 Jack's a student.
   __*Jack isn't a student.*__
2 We are Spanish.
   _____
3 The city is in Europe.
   _____
4 I'm happy.
   _____
5 Susana and Gina are from Tunisia.
   _____

4 Rewrite the sentences as questions.

1 Sydney is in Australia.
   __*Is Sydney in Australia?*__
2 You're from Egypt.
   _____
3 London is cold.
   _____
4 We're in a hotel.
   _____
5 Katya is an artist.
   _____

5 Write questions with the correct form of *be*. Then write two answers for each question with *yes* and *no*.

1 Simon / from Bolivia?
   __*Is Simon from Bolivia?*__
   __*Yes, he is.   No, he isn't.*__
2 you / on vacation?
   _____
   _____
3 your hotel / nice?
   _____
   _____
4 Susana and Gina / in Paris?
   _____
   _____

6 Write *a* or *an*.

1 I'm __*a*__ student.
2 Sonia is _____ doctor.
3 Malta is _____ island in the Mediterranean Sea.
4 This is _____ book.

7 Write the plural of these nouns.

1 a lake   _____
2 a country   _____
3 a beach   _____
4 a vacation   _____
5 an island   _____
6 an address   _____
7 a photo   _____
8 a boat   _____

GRAMMAR SUMMARY UNIT 3

his, her, its, our, their

What's	my your his her its our their	name?

Her book.

Her books.

Their book.

Their books.

What's his name?

This is my school.

This is our house.

Their children are in my class.

▶ **Exercises 1 and 2**

Possessive 's

> This is **Oscar's** car.
> **Jack's** eyes are brown.

The possessive **'s** is <u>not</u> a contraction of *is*.
    Who's Jack? = Who is Jack?
    He's my brother. = He is my brother.
    He's Maria's son. = He is Maria's son.

Oscar's car

Raul's phones

Maria's children

Fatima's cats

▶ **Exercises 3, 4, and 5**

Irregular plural nouns

a child	→	**children**
a man	→	**men**
a woman	→	**women**
a person	→	**people**

children

men

women

people

a child → *children* ✓ ~~a children~~ ✗

Add -*s* or -*es* and change -*y* to -*ies* to make regular plural nouns.

▶ **Exercise 6**

Exercises

1 Circle the correct option.

1 This is a photo of my brother in *her* / *his* car.

2 My husband is Russian. *His* / *My* name is Boris.

3 We are happy. It's *his* / *our* daughter's wedding.

4 Hi, Zara. Is this *her* / *your* mother?

5 My friends are in Spain. It's *his* / *their* vacation.

2 Complete the sentences with these words.

he	her	~~his~~	it	its	she	their	they

1 A: Robert's address is 25 Smith Road.
   B: What's ___his___ phone number?

2 A: Dani and Harry are brothers.
   B: What's _____ last name?

3 Sonia is my friend. _____'s a teacher.

4 A: What's your name?
   B: _____'s Paulo.

5 A: My son's called Riz.
   B: How old is _____ ?

6 We're from an island. _____ name is Skye.

7 Venus and Serena are tennis players. Are _____ sisters?

8 Look at Anna in _____ car.

3 Write sentences.

1 James / Oscar / father
   ___James is Oscar's father.___

2 John and James / Elena / sons
   _____

3 Lisa and Marga / John / daughters
   _____

4 Lisa / Marga / sister
   _____

5 James / Harry / son
   _____

4 Put the words in order. Write sentences with the possessive *'s*.

1 hair / Carlo / is / black
   ___Carlo's hair is black___

2 bag / this / Joana / is
   _____

3 car / the teacher / is / new
   _____

4 blue / are / eyes / Frieda
   _____

5 they / children / Nam / are
   _____

6 Michael and David / friends / are / Kim
   _____

5 Write *is* or *'s* in the correct place.

1 Who this?
   ___Who is this?___

2 My hair black.
   _____

3 How old your best friend?
   _____

4 David friends are Oscar and Paul.
   _____

5 Sandra tall.
   _____

6 Our teacher name is Andrew.
   _____

6 Complete the singular and plural nouns.

1 How old are the wom_____ in the photo?

2 Who are the pe_____ at the wedding?

3 This chil_____ is three years old.

4 Who is the pe_____ in your car?

5 James and Eliza are my chil_____ .

6 Our teacher is a m_____ .

GRAMMAR SUMMARY UNIT 4

Prepositions of place

The market is **on** Pine Street.

 The museum is **next to** the market.

The cafe is **opposite** the bus station.

The movie theater is **near** the bank.

▶ Exercises 1 and 2

this, that, these, those

This is my book.
That's your book.
These are my books.
Those are your books.

this/that = singular
these/those = plural

Use *this/these* for things near to you.
Use *that/those* for things not near to you.

▶ Exercise 3

Question words

What is that?
Where are the maps?
When is the park open?
Why is the Skytree famous?

Word order in questions with question
words = question word + *be* + subject

Affirmative form	→	Question form
It's famous.	→	**Why is it** famous?
it is	→	is it
The maps are on the table.	→	Where are the maps?
The maps are	→	are the maps

Contractions

What is	→	What's
		What's that? ✓
		~~What's it?~~ ✗
Where is	→	Where's
		Where's the car?
When is	→	When's
		When's it open?
Why is	→	Why's
		Why's it popular?

▶ Exercise 4

Exercises

1 Look at the picture of Oxford Street. Write *yes* or *no*.

1 Is the Science Museum next to the bank?
   _no_
2 Is the park on Oxford Street?
   _____
3 Is the Science Museum opposite the park?
   _____
4 Are the three people near the Science Museum?
   _____
5 Is the cafe next to the parking lot?
   _____
6 Is the Tourist Information Center opposite the bank?
   _____

2 Look at the picture of Oxford Street. Complete the sentences.

1 The bank is __next to__ the cafe.
2 The bank is _____ the Tourist Information Center.
3 The three people are _____ the park.
4 The parking lot is _____ Green's Hostel.
5 The Science Museum is _____ the parking lot.
6 The bank is _____ Oxford Street.

3 Circle the correct option.

1 Are **these** / **those** your keys?

2 **These** / **Those** buildings are old.

3 Are **these** / **those** dictionaries?

4 **These** / **Those** are my children.

5 **These** / **Those** aren't maps of Paris.

6 Are **these** / **those** lions?

4 Put the words in order to make questions.

1 is / building / what / that / ?
   What is that building?
2 is / open / the museum / when / ?
   _____
3 your friends / are / where / today / ?
   _____
4 is / why / the cafe / popular / ?
   _____

GRAMMAR SUMMARY UNIT 5

can/can't

Affirmative	
I/You He/She/It We/You/They	**can** cook.
Negative	
I/You He/She/It We/You/They	**can't** cook.

Contraction
   can't = cannot

▶ **Exercise 1**

can questions and short answers

Questions		
Can	I/you he/she/it we/you/they	cook?
Short answers		
Yes, No,	I/you he/she/it we/you/they	can. can't.

Word order in questions with *can* = *can* + subject + verb

   Affirmative form → Question form
   She can drive. → *Can she drive?*

   she can → *can she*

can = ability   *can* = request

I can speak English.

Can I have two coffees, please?

▶ **Exercises 2 and 3**

have/has

I/You We/You/They	**have**	a car. two guitars.
He/She/It	**has**	

We have a car.

Mr. and Mrs. Smith have three children.

The house has a blue door.

Susana has two guitars.

▶ **Exercise 4**

be + adjective

My car is **old**.
Your children are **beautiful**.
His camera isn't **new**.
Are these glasses **expensive**?

The adjective is the same with singular and plural subjects.
   The car is expensive.
   The glasses are expensive. ✓ ~~expensives~~. ✗

▶ **Exercise 5**

Adjective + noun

The **car** is **blue**. → It's a **blue car**.
The **photos** are **big**. → They're **big photos**.

Word order = adjective + noun, NOT noun + adjective
   I have new glasses. ✓
   I have ~~glasses new~~. ✗

▶ **Exercise 6**

Exercises

1 Circle the correct option.

1 Babies *can / can't* run.
2 Children *can / can't* see.
3 Babies *can / can't* move.
4 Cars *can / can't* fly.
5 Children *can / can't* run.
6 Animals *can / can't* speak.

2 Put the words in order to make sentences and questions.

1 play / piano / you / can / the / ?
   Can you play the piano?
2 car / drive / can't / I / a / .
   _____
3 friends / my / cook / can't / .
   _____
4 baby / walk / your / can / ?
   _____
5 can't / robot / swim / this / .
   _____
6 speak / my / Spanish / can / brother/.
   _____

3 Write questions and answers.

1 he / sing ✓
   Can he sing?
   Yes, he can.
2 you / drive a car ✓
   _____
   _____
3 they / play ping-pong ✗
   _____
   _____
4 she / cook ✗
   _____
   _____
5 they / speak English ✓
   _____
   _____
6 it / swim ✗
   _____
   _____

4 Complete the sentences with *have* or *has*.

1 I _*have*_ two cameras.
2 My brother _____ a mountain bike.
3 My friends _____ four children — they're all boys.
4 We _____ a piano.
5 My city _____ three parks.
6 My sister _____ a job. She's a teacher.

5 Write at least eight sentences with these words and *be*.

The buildings	expensive
My camera	new
Your car	popular
The museum	red
The people	tall
My sister	young

The buildings are tall.
_____
_____
_____
_____
_____
_____
_____
_____

6 Put the words in order to make sentences.

1 is / camera / this / Japanese / a
   This is a Japanese camera.
2 fantastic / phone / my / a / memory / has
   _____
3 phone / you / great / on / your / music / have
   _____
4 city / Venice / beautiful / a / is
   _____
5 blue / a / my / has / sister / car
   _____
6 is / Jack's / man / an / grandfather / old
   _____

GRAMMAR SUMMARY UNIT 6

like

Affirmative	
I	
You	
We	*like* basketball.
You	
They	

Negative	
I	
You	
We	*don't like* cycling.
You	
They	

Contraction
  don't = do not

Use *don't* with *like* to form negatives.
  Affirmative form → Negative form
  They like swimming. → *They don't like swimming.*

▸ **Exercise 1**

like questions and short answers

Questions	
Do I	
Do you	
Do we	*like* sports?
Do you	
Do they	

Short answers
Yes, I/you/we/you/they **do**.
No, I/you/we/you/they **don't**.

Use *do* with *like* to form questions.
  Affirmative form → Question form
  They like sports. → *Do they like sports?*

Short answers
  Yes, I do. ✓   *Yes, I ~~like~~.* ✗
  No, I don't. ✓   *No, I ~~don't like~~.* ✗

▸ **Exercises 2 and 3**

he/she + like

Affirmative	
He	
She	*likes* books.

Negative	
He	
She	*doesn't like* music.

Contraction
  doesn't = does not

Questions		
Does	he	*like* fish?
	she	

Short answers
Yes, he/she **does**.
No, he/she **doesn't**.

Use *doesn't* or *does* with *like* to form negatives and questions.
  He doesn't like TV.
  Does she like animals?

Short answers
  Yes, he does. ✓   *Yes, ~~he likes~~.*
                       Yes, he ~~does like~~. ✗
  No, she doesn't. ✓   *No, she ~~doesn't like~~.* ✗

▸ **Exercises 4 and 5**

Object pronouns

	me.
	you.
	him.
	her.
Diana likes	**it.**
	us.
	you.
	them.

Subject pronouns are before the verb.
  I/you/he/she/it/we/you/they like(s) Diana.

Object pronouns are after the verb.
  Diana likes me/you/him/her/it/us/you/them.

▸ **Exercise 6**

Exercises

1 Write sentences with the correct form of *like*.

1 I / basketball ☹

    I don't like basketball.

2 we / baseball ☺

    _____

3 they / tennis ☺

    _____

4 you / swimming ☹

    _____

5 I / London ☺

    _____

6 they / coffee ☹

    _____

2 Write questions with the words. Then write answers to the questions.

1 Formula 1 / they ✓

    Do they like Formula 1?

    Yes, they do.

2 soccer / you ✗

    _____

    _____

3 animals / you ✓

    _____

    _____

4 the beach / they ✗

    _____

    _____

3 Rewrite the sentences in the form given in parentheses.

1 I like motorcycles. (negative)

    I don't like motorcycles.

2 Your friends like cats. (question)

    _____

3 You don't like cities. (affirmative)

    _____

4 We don't like running. (affirmative)

    _____

5 We like soccer. (negative)

    _____

4 Write sentences with the correct form of *like*.

1 Toni / music ☺

    Toni likes music.

2 Ahmed / detective stories ☹

    _____

3 Elena / animals ☺

    _____

4 Kim / cold places ☹

    _____

5 Tanya / beaches ☺

    _____

6 Nuno / fish ☹

    _____

5 Four of these sentences have a missing word: *does* or *doesn't*. Rewrite the four sentences with the missing word.

1 Nam likes New York.

    _____

2 Joanna like movies.

    _____

3 your teacher like music?

    _____

4 Stefan like swimming.

    _____

5 Elise like sports?

    _____

6 Krishnan likes wildlife shows.

    _____

6 Look at the <u>underlined</u> nouns. Complete the sentences with an object pronoun.

1 I like <u>wildlife shows</u>, but my friend doesn't like *them* .

2 <u>We</u> can't see you. Can you see _____ ?

3 <u>She</u>'s a popular writer, but I don't like _____ .

4 A: Do you like <u>pop music</u>?
   B: Yes, I love _____ .

5 <u>Matt Damon</u> is fantastic in the *Bourne* movies. I love _____ .

6 <u>I</u> have a cat. It loves _____ .

GRAMMAR SUMMARY UNIT 7

Simple present *I/you/we/ you/they*

Affirmative		
I		
You		
We	**get up**	at six o'clock.
You		
They		

Negative		
I		
You		
We	**don't get up**	at six o'clock.
You		
They		

Contraction
  don't = do not

Use *don't* with the simple present to form negatives.

  Affirmative form → Negative form
  They speak English. → *They don't speak English.*

Use the simple present to talk about routines.
  We watch TV in the evening.

Use the simple present to talk about true things.
  I have two children.

▸ **Exercises 1 and 2**

Prepositions of time

at six o'clock

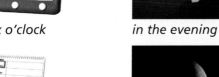

in the evening

on Monday/Mondays   at night

▸ **Exercise 3**

Simple present questions *I/you/we/you/they*

Questions			
	I		
	you		
Do	we	**play** tennis?	
	you		
	they		

Short answers
Yes, I/you/we/you/they **do**.
No, I/you/we/you/they **don't**.

Use *do* with the simple present to form questions.

  Affirmative form → Question form
  They live in Boston. → *Do they live in Boston?* ✓
  → ~~*They live in Boston?*~~ ✗

Short answers
  Yes, they do. ✓   *Yes, they* ~~*live*~~. ✗
  No, they don't. ✓   *No, they* ~~*don't live*~~. ✗

▸ **Exercises 4 and 5**

Simple present *Wh-* questions

What			
Where			**do?**
Who	**do**	I/you/we/you/they	**go?**
Why			**meet?**
When			

Word order in simple present *Wh-* questions
= *Wh-* word + *do* + subject + verb

Simple present questions and *Wh-* questions:
Affirmative =   *They work.*
Question =   *Do   they work?*
Wh- question = *Where   do   they work?*

▸ **Exercise 6**

Exercises

1 Rewrite the sentences in the form given in parentheses

1 I have breakfast at seven o'clock. (negative)

   I don't have breakfast at seven o'clock.

2 You don't watch TV in the evening. (affirmative)

   _____

3 My friends start work at nine o'clock. (negative)

   _____

4 I don't have classes on Fridays. (affirmative)

   _____

5 We finish class at eight o'clock. (negative)

   _____

6 They go to bed at midnight. (negative)

   _____

2 Write sentences with these verbs.

not eat	not get up	have
study	~~watch~~	

1 I / TV

   I watch TV.

2 you / English

   _____

3 they / lunch in a cafe

   _____

4 my friends / meat

   _____

5 I / at eight o'clock

   _____

3 Circle the correct preposition.

1 We don't go to class *at / on* Saturdays and Sundays.
2 They eat cereal *in / on* the morning.
3 I don't drink coffee *at / in* the evening.
4 I finish work *at / in* seven o'clock.
5 You sleep *at / in* night.

4 Write questions with the words. Then write answers to the questions.

1 every week (you / climb) ✓

   Do you climb every week?
   Yes, we do.

2 soccer (they / play) ✗

   _____
   _____

3 cakes (you / make) ✓

   _____
   _____

4 in a band (your friends / sing) ✓

   _____
   _____

5 shopping (you / enjoy) ✓

   _____
   _____

5 Write sentences and questions with the words in parentheses.

1 you / painting / ? (like)

   Do you like painting?

2 My friends / German / . (not speak)

   _____

3 you / to music / ? (listen)

   _____

4 We / the guitar / . (not play)

   _____

5 they / dinner every evening / ? (cook)

   _____

6 Put the words in order to make questions.

1 to the beach / do / go / when / you / ?

   When do you go to the beach?

2 do / they / what / at the beach / do / ?

   _____

3 with / do / you / who / sing / ?

   _____

4 go / swimming / where / they / do / ?

   _____

5 you / like / why / do / running / ?

   _____

Simple present he/she/it

Affirmative		
He She	**drives**	a train.
It	**opens**	at ten o'clock.
Negative		
He She	**doesn't drive**	a bus.
It	**doesn't open**	at nine o'clock.

Spelling changes

Add -s to the base form of the verb.

   drive → *drives*

Add -es to verbs that end in -ch and -sh.

   teach → *teaches*
   finish → *finishes*

The verbs *do, go,* and *have* are irregular.

   do → *does*
   go → *goes*
   have → *has*

He drives a train.

It doesn't open at nine o'clock.

▶ **Exercises 1, 2, and 3**

Simple present questions he/she/it

Questions		
Does	he she it	**teach?** **work?**
Short answers		
Yes, he/she/it **does.**		
No, he/she/it **doesn't.**		

Wh- questions			
What **Where**	**does**	he she it	**do?** **go?**

Use *does* + *he / she / it* + the simple present to form questions.

   Affirmative form → Question form
   She works in a park. → *Does she work in a park?* ✓

Short answers

   Yes, she does. ✓   *Yes, she ~~works~~.* ✗
   No, she doesn't. ✓   *No, she ~~doesn't work~~.* ✗

▶ **Exercises 4 and 5**

Frequency adverbs

0%

   *My friend **never** writes emails.*
   *I **sometimes** travel in my job.*
   *We **usually** get up early.*
   *My friend **often** works late.*
   *I **always** have breakfast.*

100%

Word order with frequency adverbs:
adverb + verb

   He often watches TV.

be + adverb

   I am often late. ✓ *I ~~often am~~ late.* ✗

Use *never* with affirmative verbs.

   She never gets up early. ✓
   She ~~never doesn't get up~~ early. ✗

▶ **Exercise 6**

Exercises

1 Complete the sentences with the correct form of the verbs in parentheses.

1 Jack _works_ (work) in a hospital.
2 Ryan _____ (serve) customers in a cafe.
3 The bus _____ (not / stop) near my house.
4 This button _____ (open) the doors.
5 Kristen _____ (not / walk) to work every day.

2 Complete the paragraph with the correct form of these verbs.

buy	get	go	have	play
use	watch	~~work~~	not work	sell

Alain Bofill ¹ _works_ in the city. He
² _____ a computer all day. He
³ _____ and ⁴ _____
money—dollars, pounds, and euros. He
⁵ _____ home on the subway. He
⁶ _____ home at nine o'clock in the
evening. He ⁷ _____ dinner and he
⁸ _____ TV. He ⁹ _____ on
Saturdays—he ¹⁰ _____ golf with his
friends.

3 Rewrite the sentences in the form given in parentheses.

1 Your friend lives near a beach. (negative)
   Your friend doesn't live near a beach.
2 Ahmed doesn't drive to work. (affirmative)
   _____
3 My sister enjoys her job. (negative)
   _____
4 The office opens on Sundays. (negative)
   _____
5 He doesn't watch videos at work. (affirmative)
   _____

4 Write questions with the words in parentheses.

1 Simon / Arabic? (understand)
   Does Simon understand Arabic?
2 Anne / German? (speak)
   _____
3 Lin / near you? (live)
   _____
4 Boris / in the evening? (study)
   _____
5 your friend / English? (teach)
   _____

5 Read the sentences. Then write questions with the words in parentheses.

1 Carl doesn't finish work at eight o'clock. (nine o'clock?)
   Does he finish work at nine o'clock?
2 Jon doesn't work in an office. (where?)
   _____
3 Julia doesn't goes to bed late. (early?)
   _____
4 My brother doesn't read novels. (what?)
   _____
5 My sister doesn't like tea. (coffee?)
   _____

6 Put the words in order to make sentences.

1 coffee / have / usually / I
   _____
2 travels / colleague / my / in her job / often
   _____
3 homework / never / our / gives / teacher / us
   _____
4 studies / my / at home / friend / sometimes
   _____
5 always / I / at night / read
   _____
6 my / brother / late / always / works
   _____

GRAMMAR SUMMARY UNIT 9

there is/are

Singular
There's a book in my bag.
There's a camera on my phone.

Plural
There are some books in my bag.
There are two computers in my office.

Contraction
> *there's = there is*

> *There's a camera on my phone.*
> *= My phone has a camera.*

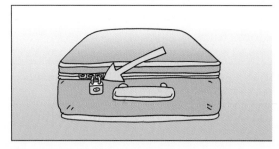

There's a lock on the suitcase.

There's a virus on my computer!

There are some tables near the window.

There are twenty houses on my street.

▶ **Exercises 1 and 2**

there is/are negative and question forms

Negative singular
There isn't a fridge in the room.

Negative plural
There aren't any hotels here.

Contractions
> *there isn't = there is not*
> *there aren't = there are not*

Use *a* after *there isn't*.
Use *any* after *there aren't*.

Singular question forms	
Is there a couch?	Yes, **there is.**
	No, **there isn't.**

Plural question forms	
Are there any trains today?	Yes, **there are.**
	No, **there aren't.**

Affirmative form	→ Question form
There's a couch.	→ *Is there a couch?*
there is	→ *is there*
There are some books.	→ *Are there any books?*
there are	→ *are there*

Use *a* after *Is there*.
Use *any* after *Are there*.

Short answers
> *Yes, there is.* ✓   *Yes, ~~there's.~~* ✗

▶ **Exercises 3, 4, and 5**

Imperative forms

Buy your tickets online.
Don't travel by train.

The imperative is the base form of the verb. The negative is *Don't* + base form.

Imperatives are the same when you speak to one person or more than one person.

▶ **Exercise 6**

Exercises

1 Write *a* or *some* in the correct place.

1 There are pens in my bag.
   There are some pens in my bag.

2 There's tablet on my desk.
   _____

3 There are shirts in my suitcase.
   _____

4 There are people on this plane.
   _____

5 There's scarf in my hand.
   _____

2 Look at the picture. Write sentences with the words.

1 a map
   There's a map.
2 keys
   _____
3 books
   _____
4 a camera
   _____
5 a passport
   _____

3 Write questions with the words. Then look at the picture in Exercise 2 again and write answers to the questions.

1 a map
   Is there a map?   Yes, there is.

2 a phone
   _____

3 pens
   _____

4 a passport
   _____

5 keys
   _____

4 Complete the conversation with the correct forms of *there is / are*.

A: Let's go to Loch Ness for the New Year.
B: ¹ _____ an airport near Loch Ness?
A: Yes, ² _____ .
B: ³ _____ any flights from here?
A: ⁴ _____ flights Mondays to Fridays, but ⁵ _____ any flights on weekends.
B: OK. Let's go there on Friday.

5 Write *a* or *any* in the correct place.

1 Are there chairs in the room?
   Are there any chairs in the room?
2 There aren't bottles in the fridge.
   _____
3 Is there shower in the hotel room?
   _____
4 There isn't train station in this town.
   _____

6 Read the instructions from a tour guide. Circle the best option.

1 *Don't forget / Forget* your passports.
2 *Don't arrive / Arrive* at the airport on time.
3 *Don't give / Give* me your cell phone numbers, please.
4 *Don't wait / Wait* a moment, please.

GRAMMAR SUMMARY UNIT 10

be: was/were

Affirmative		
I/He/She/It	**was**	Russian.
You/We/You/They	**were**	

Use *was* and *were* to talk about the past.

is ➔ *was*   *are* ➔ *were*

Edurne is an explorer.
She was born in 1973.

Albert Einstein was
German.

The Beatles were English.

▶ **Exercises 1 and 2**

be: was/were negative and question forms

Negative		
I/He/She/It	**wasn't**	famous.
You/We/You/They	**weren't**	

Contractions

wasn't = was not   *weren't = were not*

Questions		
Was	I/he/she/it	happy?
Were	you/we/you/they	on TV?

Short answers
Yes, I/he/she/it **was**.
No, I/he/she/it **wasn't**.
Yes, you/we/you/they **were**.
No, you/we/you/they **weren't**.

Affirmative form ➔ Question form
It was 1956.   ➔ *Was it 1956?*

it was   ➔ *was it*

▶ **Exercises 3, 4, and 5**

Regular simple past verbs

Affirmative	
I	
You	
He	
She	
It	*lived from 1480 to 1521.*
We	
You	
They	

Use the simple past to talk about the past.
   Magellan was an explorer. He lived from 1480 to 1521.

Regular simple past verbs end in *-ed*. The form is the same for *I/you/he/she/it/we/you/they*.

live   ➔   *lived*

Some regular simple past verbs are:

checked	*opened*	*used*
closed	*started*	*visited*
enjoyed	*studied*	*walked*
finished	*traveled*	*watched*
liked	*tried*	*worked*

Spelling changes
Add *-ed* to the base form.

start   ➔   *started*
watch   ➔   *watched*

Add *-d*.

live   ➔   *lived*
use   ➔   *used*

Change *-y* after a consonant to *-ied*.

study   ➔   *studied*

▶ **Exercise 6**

Exercises

1 Put the words in order to make sentences.

1 was / the first / Neil Armstrong / on the moon / person
   Neil Armstrong was the first person on the moon.

2 was / Ayrton Senna / racing driver / a
   _____
   _____

3 parents / born / my / in Zurich / were
   _____
   _____

4 and Magellan / Drake / leaders / were / expedition
   _____
   _____

5 musician / a / John Lennon / was
   _____
   _____

2 Complete the paragraph with *was* or *were*.

Sally Ride [1] _____ the first American woman in space. She [2] _____ born in 1951. Her parents [3] _____ from California. Her first space flight [4] _____ in 1983. She [5] _____ the writer of five books for children. They [6] _____ about space and science.

3 Rewrite the sentences in the form given in parentheses.

1 Joe's favorite teacher was Mr. Lee. (question)
   Was Joe's favorite teacher Mr. Lee?

2 I wasn't at home yesterday. (affirmative)
   _____

3 Tran's parents weren't TV presenters. (question)
   _____

4 David Attenborough's TV shows were about sports. (negative)
   _____

5 Were they good students at school? (negative)
   _____

4 Complete the sentences with *was*, *wasn't*, *were*, and *weren't*.

1 A: _____ Sesame Street your favorite TV show?
   B: No, it _____ .

2 A: Who _____ your best friends at school?
   B: They _____ Angela and Lia.

3 My mother _____ the first woman in our family with a college degree.

4 A: _____ your teachers at school nice?
   B: Yes, they _____ .

5 A: _____ the first Olympic Games in Athens?
   B: No, they _____ . They _____ in Olympia.

5 Read the answers. Then write *was* or *were* questions.

1 John Lennon wasn't born in Manchester.
   Was John Lennon born in Manchester?

2 Victoria wasn't the first British queen.
   _____

3 Sal's sister wasn't born in 2001.
   _____

4 Nina's grandparents weren't from Hong Kong.
   _____

5 Olga's uncle was famous.
   _____

6 Teo's parents weren't born in Europe.
   _____

6 Write the simple past form of the verbs.

1 My grandfather _died_ (die) in 2006.
2 I _____ (live) in Rome from 2014 to 2017.
3 My mother _____ (study) science in college.
4 James _____ (work) in a cafe in 2016.
5 We _____ (visit) Florida last summer.

GRAMMAR SUMMARY UNIT 11

Irregular simple past verbs

Affirmative	
I/You He/She/It We/You/They	**went** to the Alps. **had** a good vacation.

Use the simple past to talk about the past.

Regular simple past verbs end with *-ed*. Irregular simple past verbs do not end with *-ed*.

be	→	*was/were*	*have*	→	*had*
buy	→	*bought*	*leave*	→	*left*
come	→	*came*	*make*	→	*made*
do	→	*did*	*meet*	→	*met*
drive	→	*drove*	*see*	→	*saw*
eat	→	*ate*	*speak*	→	*spoke*
find	→	*found*	*take*	→	*took*
go	→	*went*	*write*	→	*wrote*

The form is the same for *I/you/he/she/it/we/you/they.*

In 2013

We went to Thailand.

In 2014

We saw the Pyramids.

In 2015

We ate pizza in Naples.

In 2016

We bought a house.

▶ **Exercises 1, 2, and 3**

Simple past negative and question forms

Negative	
I/You He/She/It We/You/They	**didn't visit** Paris last summer. **didn't go** on vacation last year.

Questions		
	I/you	**visit** Paris last summer?
Did	*he/she/it*	**go** on vacation last
	we/you/they	year?

Short answers
Yes, I/you/he/she/it/we/you/they **did**. No, I/you/he/she/it/we/you/they **didn't**.

Contraction
  didn't = did not

Use the base form of verbs in simple past negative and question forms.

  We watched TV. → *We didn't watch TV.* ✓
  We ~~didn't watched~~ TV last night. ✗

  Did you watch TV last night? ✓
  Did ~~you watched~~ TV last night? ✗

▶ **Exercises 4 and 5**

Simple past *Wh-* questions

Wh- questions			
What			**do?**
Where		*I/you*	**go?**
When	**did**	*he/she/it*	**leave?**
Why		*we/you/they*	**stop?**
Who			**see?**

Word order in simple past *Wh-* questions
= *Wh-* word + *did* + subject + verb

Simple past questions and *Wh-* questions:

Affirmative =			*They stopped.*
Question =		*Did*	*they stop?*
Wh- question =	*Why*	*did*	*they stop?*

▶ **Exercise 6**

Exercises

1 Complete the sentences with the simple past form of the verbs.

1. We __took__ (take) a lot of photos on our vacation.
2. The tourists _____ (go) to all the popular places.
3. I _____ (have) lunch with my friends yesterday.
4. We _____ (see) a great movie last week.
5. I _____ (make) dinner for my family last night.
6. My father _____ (leave) school when he was fourteen.

2 Write sentences about things that happened yesterday with the simple past form of the verbs.

buy	come	drive	make	speak

1. my friends / to my house
   ___My friends came to my house.___
2. I / lunch in my kitchen
   _____
3. we / to the mall
   _____
4. my parents / their plane tickets
   _____
5. I / to my sister on Skype
   _____

3 Complete the text with the simple past form of the verbs.

Last weekend, we [1] _____ (go) for a walk in the mountains. We [2] _____ (start) early in the morning. We [3] _____ (walk) for two hours. Then we [4] _____ (have) a snack. We [5] _____ (find) a bag on the walk. We [6] _____ (finish) our walk and we [7] _____ (take) the bag to the police station. The police [8] _____ (find) a lot of money in the bag.

4 Rewrite the sentences in the form given in parentheses.

1. I didn't go to college. (affirmative)
   I went to college.
2. We ate burgers yesterday. (negative)
   _____
3. Shakespeare wrote a lot of plays. (question)
   _____
4. I lived with my grandparents when I was a child. (negative)
   _____
5. Tony didn't meet his wife at work. (affirmative)
   _____

5 Complete the interview with a travel writer.

Q: [1] _____ (you / travel) a lot last year?
A: Yes, I [2] _____ . I went to three continents.
Q: Wow! [3] _____ (you / go) to South America?
A: Yes, I did. I went with a friend. We visited Ecuador, Peru, and Chile, but we [4] _____ (not / have) time to go to Argentina.
Q: [5] _____ (you / write) a book about your trip?
A: No, I [6] _____ , but I wrote a blog and I made some videos about it.

6 Write *Wh-* questions for these answers. Use the correct form of the underlined verbs.

1. We <u>met</u> lots of interesting people.
   Who did you meet?
2. They <u>went</u> to Cancun in Mexico.
   _____
3. She <u>saw</u> some beautiful buildings.
   _____
4. We <u>arrived</u> at the hotel at night.
   _____
5. I <u>went</u> there because I like the food.
   _____

GRAMMAR SUMMARY UNIT 12

Present continuous

Affirmative

I	am	cooking.
He/She/It	is	eating.
We/You/They	are	reading.

Negative

I	am not	cooking.
He/She/It	isn't	eating.
We/You/They	aren't	reading.

Use *be* (auxiliary verb) + the *-ing* form of the verb to make the present continuous.

We are / We're cooking.

Contractions

I am cooking.	→	*I'm cooking.*
He is reading.	→	*He's reading.*
They are sleeping.	→	*They're sleeping.*

Use the present continuous for activities in progress at the time of speaking.

We're cooking.

She's reading. She isn't watching TV.

▶ **Exercises 1 and 2**

Present continuous questions and short answers

Questions

Am	I	
Is	he/she/it	reading?
Are	we/you/they	

Short answers

	I	am.
Yes,	he/she/it	is.
	we/you/they	are.
	I	am not.
No,	he/she/it	isn't.
	we/you/they	aren't.

Wh- questions

What	*are* we/you/they	*doing?*
Where	*is* he/she/it	*going?*

Word order in present continuous questions = (*Wh-*) + *be* + subject + *-ing*

Affirmative =			*They're playing.*
Question =		*Are*	*they playing?*
Wh- question =	*What*	*are*	*they playing?*

What are you doing?

I'm having a cup of coffee.

▶ **Exercises 3 and 4**

Present continuous for the future

I'm meeting my friends	**tomorrow.**
	on Sunday morning.
	this/next weekend.
	on June 8th.

Use the present continuous + future time expressions for future plans.

We're flying to Rome on June 15th.

▶ **Exercise 5**

Prepositions of place

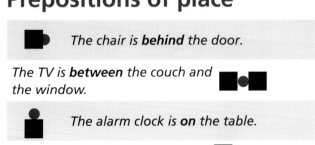

The chair is **behind** the door.

The TV is **between** the couch and the window.

The alarm clock is **on** the table.

The table is **under** the window.

▶ **Exercise 6**

Exercises

1 Look at the picture of the classroom. Complete the sentences with the correct form of the verbs in parentheses.

1 The teacher _is talking_ (talk) to Leon
2 Leon _____ (listen) to the teacher.
3 Amy and Roy _____ (write).
4 Paula _____ (read).
5 The students at the back _____ (watch) a video.
6 Olga _____ (look) out the window.

2 Write the sentences in Exercise 1 in the negative form.

1 _The teacher isn't talking to Leon._
2 _____
3 _____
4 _____
5 _____
6 _____

3 Write questions with these words. Write short answers.

1 you / listen / to me ✓
   Are you listening to me?
   Yes, I am.
2 Jenni / make coffee ✓
   _____
   _____
3 the movie / start ✗
   _____
   _____
4 the children / play soccer ✓
   _____
   _____
5 you / watch this TV show ✗
   _____
   _____
6 David / wash his car ✗
   _____
   _____

4 Rewrite the sentences in the form given in parentheses.

1 They're making lunch. (question)
   _____
2 He's reading the newspaper. (negative)
   _____
3 We aren't washing the car. (affirmative)
   _____
4 You aren't eating. (question)
   _____
5 Is she sitting on the floor? (negative)
   _____

5 Read the sentences. Do they refer to now (N) or the future (F)?

1 I'm playing tennis on Sunday. ___
2 We aren't listening to the radio. ___
3 My friends are coming this weekend. ___
4 Is your family having dinner together tonight? ___
5 What are you doing in June? ___
6 My sister is staying with us. ___

6 Read the sentences about things in a living room. Circle the correct option.

1 The couch is *between / under* the door and the window.
2 There's a cabinet *between / behind* the couch.
3 The clock is *between / on* two windows.
4 There are some flowers *behind / on* the desk.
5 There's a rug *on / under* the table

Unit 1

▶ 1

Hello! I'm David.

▶ 2

1 D: Hello. I'm David.
   M: Hi. I'm Mireya.
   D: Mireya Mayor?
   M: Yes.
2 D: Hi! I'm David Doubilet.
   M: Hello.
   D: Oh! You're Mireya!
   M: Yes. I'm Mireya Mayor.
3 D: Hello. I'm David Doubilet.
   M: I'm Mireya.
   D: Mireya?
   M: Yes. M–I–R–E–Y–A.
   D: Hi. Nice to meet you.

▶ 6

1 P: I'm Paula.
   Q: Can you spell Paula?
   P: Yes. P–A–U–L–A.
2 B: I'm Bryan.
   Q: Can you spell Bryan?
   B: Yes. B–R–Y–A–N.
3 S: I'm Simon.
   Q: Can you spell Simon?
   S: Yes. S–I–M–O–N.
4 A: I'm Anna.
   Q: Can you spell Anna?
   A: Yes. A–double N–A.

▶ 9

1	Brazil	Brazilian
2	Egypt	Egyptian
3	Italy	Italian
4	Mexico	Mexican
5	Spain	Spanish
6	the United Kingdom	British
7	the United States	American
8	Vietnam	Vietnamese

▶ 14

1 Baseball is American.
2 Pasta is from Italy.
3 Jaguar is British.
4 Flamenco is from Spain.

▶ 15

I = interviewer

I: Anne-Marie, what's your phone number?
A: It's 555 760 7101.
I: 5–5–5, 7–6–0, 7–1–0–1. OK?
A: Yes.
I: Thanks.

▶ 16

I = interviewer

I: Nelson, what's your phone number?

N: My work number is 555 736 3100.
I: 5–5–5, 7–3–6, 3–double 1–0?
N: No, it's 3 –1–double 0.
I: OK. Thanks. What's your home number?
N: My home number is 555 340 2583.
I: 5–5–5, 3–4–0, 2–5–8–3. Thanks.

▶ 17

Hi.
Hello.
Good morning.
Good afternoon.
Good evening.
Good night.
Goodbye.
Bye.
See you later.

▶ 19

1 S: What's this in English?
   T: It's a bag.
   S: Can you spell it?
   T: Yes. B–A–G. Bag.
   S: Thanks.
2 S: What's this in English?
   T: It's a classroom.
   S: Can you spell classroom?
   T: Yes. C–L–A–double S–R–double O–M. Classroom.
   S: Thanks.
3 S: What's this in English?
   T: It's a computer.
   S: Can you spell it?
   T: Yes. C–O–M–P–U–T–E–R. Computer.
   S: Thanks.
4 S: What's this in English?
   T: It's a notebook.
   S: Can you spell notebook?
   T: Yes. N–O–T–E–B–double O–K. Notebook.
   S: Thanks.
5 S: What's this in English?
   T: It's a pen.
   S: Can you spell it?
   T: Yes. P–E–N. Pen.
   S: Thanks.
6 S: What's this in English?
   T: It's a pencil.
   S: Can you spell it?
   T: Yes. P–E–N–C–I–L. Pencil.
   S: Thanks.
7 S: What's this in English?
   T: It's a phone.
   S: Can you spell phone?
   T: Yes. P–H–O–N–E. Phone.
   S: Thanks.

8 S: What's this in English?
   T: It's a table.
   S: Can you spell it?
   T: Yes. T–A–B–L–E. Table.
   S: Thanks.

▶ 21

1 T: Good afternoon, everyone. Sit down, please.
2 T: OK. Open your books. Look at page six.
3 S1: Hello. Sorry I'm late.
   T: That's OK. Sit down, please.
4 S2: Can you repeat that, please?
   T: Yes. Look at page six.
5 T: Work in pairs.
   S3: I don't understand.
   T: Work in pairs—two students.
6 T: This is a computer.
   S4: Can you spell it, please?
7 S2: What's this in English?
   T: It's a phone.
   S2: Thanks.
8 T: Do Exercise 7 at home. See you next time.
   S1 & S3: Bye.

▶ 22

Can you repeat that, please?
Can you spell it, please?
What's this in English?

Unit 2

▶ 23

This is in Vietnam. It's a river. It's morning.

▶ 25

1 Monday
2 Tuesday
3 Wednesday
4 Thursday
5 Friday
6 Saturday
7 Sunday

▶ 27

1 This is Jane. This is Paul. They're Australian.
2 I'm Meera. This is Suri. We're from India.
3 In this photo, I'm with my friend Jack. We're in Egypt.
4 Laura is with Brad, Andy, and Jessica. They're on vacation.

▶ 28

1 They're Australian.
2 We're from India.
3 We're in Egypt.
4 They're on vacation.

▶ 29
1 We aren't in Tunisia.
2 It isn't a beach.
3 Brad isn't on a camel.
4 I'm not in this photo.

▶ 31
zero
ten
twenty
thirty
forty
fifty
sixty
seventy
eighty
ninety
one hundred

▶ 32
1 four
2 twenty-three, twenty-nine, sixteen, eleven
3 sixteen, forty-five

▶ 33
a It isn't hot. It's thirteen degrees.
b Phew! It's cold this morning! It's two degrees.
c It's twenty-nine degrees in Casablanca today. And it's eleven degrees in Copenhagen.

▶ 34
1 It's six degrees in Seoul today. It's cold.
2 It's thirty-five degrees in Sydney today. It's hot.
3 It's nineteen degrees in Lima today. It's warm.

▶ 35
G = Greg, L = Lorna
G: Hi! Where are you now? Are you in France?
L: Yes, I am. I'm in the Alps. It's beautiful!
G: Are Kara and Ona there, too?
L: No, they aren't. They're on a beach in Morocco!
G: Oh, OK. Is it cold in the Alps?
L: Yes, it is. It's two degrees!
G: Wow! Are you OK?
L: Yes, I am. I'm in the hotel. It's warm here.
G: That's good. It's thirty-six degrees in Sydney today.
L: Oh! That's hot!

▶ 36
1 Q: Are you OK?
   A: Yes, I am.

2 Q: Is Kara in France?
   A: No, she isn't.
3 Q: Are you and Paul in Sydney?
   A: Yes, we are.
4 Q: Are Kara and Ona in Morocco?
   A: Yes, they are.
5 Q: Is your watch nice?
   A: Yes, it is.

▶ 38
1 In London, buses are red.
2 In Hawaii, beaches are black.
3 Cuba is an island.
4 In Cuba, cars are old.
5 In Iceland, lakes are hot.
6 Lake Geneva is in two countries— Switzerland and France.
7 The Blue Mountains are in Australia.
8 Beijing, Shanghai, and Guangzhou are cities in China.
9 O'Hare is an airport in Chicago.

▶ 40
1 books
2 students
3 dresses
4 desks
5 cities
6 watches

▶ 41
1 My car license plate number is PT61 APR.
2 My email address is jamesp@edu.au.
3 My address is 154 Westwood Avenue, Los Angeles, California 90024.
4 Here are your keys.

▶ 42
A = assistant, L = Ms. Lopez
A: Good evening.
L: Good evening. My name's Lopez. My car booking is for three days— Tuesday to Thursday.
A: Ah yes, Ms. Lopez. What's your first name, please?
L: It's Marta. Here's my ID—Marta is my first name. Lopez is my last name.
A: Thank you. Where are you from in Mexico, Ms. Lopez?
L: I'm from Mexico City.
A: Ah! Is this your address?
L: Yes, it is.
A: OK. Are you here on vacation?
L: No, I'm not. I'm on business.
A: What's your email address, please?
L: It's m lopez at daymail dot com
A: OK. Here are your keys. The car is in the parking lot.
L: Thanks. What's the car license plate number?

A: It's on your key—UGM 96B.
L: Thanks.

Unit 3

▶ 48
A: Is this a photo of your family?
B: Yes, it is.
A: Who's this?
B: She's my sister. Her name's Heelan. It's her wedding.
A: OK. So is this her husband?
B: Yes. His name's Husham.
A: Is this your daughter?
B: Yes. Her name's Nadia.
A: How old is she?
B: She's twelve years old.

▶ 49
Three important people in my life are Elisa, Nuno, and Prem.
Elisa's my best friend. She's twenty-three. Elisa's eyes are brown and her hair is black. She's tall. She's nice.
Nuno is my brother. He's my friend, too. He's twenty-five years old. My eyes are brown, but Nuno's eyes are green. His hair is brown. He isn't tall. We're both short.
Prem is a friend in my English class. Prem's eyes are brown. His hair is brown, too. He's young—he's seventeen!

▶ 50
1 Ana is Nuno's sister.
2 Prem is Ana's classmate.
3 Ana's eyes are brown.
4 Prem's school is The English Academy.
5 Ana's friends are Elisa and Prem.

▶ 51
1 January
2 February
3 March
4 April
5 May
6 June
7 July
8 August
9 September
10 October
11 November
12 December

▶ 54
My name is Kyle. There are many people in my family. These are my brothers and sisters. Mark and Peter are my younger brothers. They are children. Daniel and David are my older brothers. They are men. Sofia and Camila are my sisters. They are women.

▶ 56

A: Congratulations!

B: Thank you. We're very happy.

A: What's her name?

B: It's Juba.

A: Hello, Juba.

▶ 57

1 D = Diana, E = Edward

E: Hello!

D: Hello, Edward. Come in.

E: Happy New Year!

D: Happy New Year to you too! Come and say hello to my family.

2 F = Freya, G = Gloria

G: Happy Birthday, Freya.

F: Thank you.

G: How old are you? Nineteen or twenty?

F: Actually, I'm twenty-one.

G: Oh, great! When's the party?

F: It's on Saturday.

3 A = Adam, E = Emma, J = James

A: Congratulations, Emma and James!

E & J: Thank you very much.

A: I'm very happy for you. Here's a card and a gift for you.

E: Thank you!

A: Your dress is beautiful, Emma!

E: Thanks.

▶ 59

C = Celia, E = Elena

C: Hello, Elena. It's nice to see you. Come in.

E: Hi, Celia. This is for the baby.

C: Oh, that's very kind. Thank you very much.

E: You're welcome. Now, where *is* the baby?

C: She's with my mom.

Unit 4

▶ 61

Kazakhstan is in Asia. The new capital city of Kazakhstan is called Astana. The word "Astana" means "capital" in the Kazakh language. The buildings in Astana are tall and new. At night, they are different colors—red, blue, purple, yellow, and green. Astana is a clean and modern city. Tourists visit the parks in Astana.

▶ 62

1 a park

2 a parking lot

3 a cafe

4 a market

5 an information center

6 a bus station

7 a train station

8 a bank

9 a museum

10 a movie theater

▶ 63

1 A: Excuse me?

B: Yes?

A: Where's the train station?

B: It's on Clay Street.

A: Is it near here?

B: Yes, it is.

A: OK. Thanks.

2 C: Excuse me?

D: Yes?

C: Is the information center near here?

D: Yes, it is. It's near the park.

C: OK. Thanks.

3 E: Excuse me?

F: Yes?

E: Is the parking lot on this street?

F: No, it isn't. This is Clay Street. The parking lot's on Bush Street. It's next to the park.

E: Thank you very much.

4 G: Excuse me?

H: Yes?

G: Where's the bank?

H: I'm not sure. Oh! It's opposite the museum.

G: Is it near here?

H: Yes, it is.

G: OK. Thanks.

▶ 64

T = tourist, A = Tourist Information Center assistant

1 T1: Hi.

A: Good morning.

T1: Is this a map of New York?

A: No. That's the wrong map. This is a map of New York.

T1: Oh, OK. Where's the Guggenheim Museum?

A: It's near Fifth Avenue ... here it is.

2 T2: Good afternoon. Where are the schedules, please?

A: Well, these are train schedules, here.

T2: And bus schedules?

A: Those are bus schedules, next to the door.

T2: OK, thanks.

▶ 65

1 A: Is this a train schedule?

B: No, it's a bus schedule.

2 A: Excuse me. Are these pens or pencils?

B: They're pencils. The pens are next to the maps.

3 A: Excuse me. Are those maps of Astana?

B: Yes, they are.

4 A: Is that guidebook in English?

B: Which guidebook?

A: The book next to you.

B: No, it isn't. It's in Spanish.

▶ 68

1 It's eleven o'clock.

2 It's nine thirty.

3 It's eight twenty.

4 It's three fifty-five.

▶ 69

1 A: Where are your children? Are they here?

B: No. It's 10 a.m. They're at school.

2 A: Sandy, what time is your train?

B: It's at five o'clock.

3 A: Hi Tom. Are you at work?

B: No, I'm not. It's a holiday today. I'm at home.

▶ 71

a water

b fruit juice

c coffee

d salad

e tea

f sandwich

g apple

h banana

▶ 72

1 A: Hi. Can I help you?

C: Two coffees, please.

A: Large or small?

C: Small.

A: Anything else?

C: No, thanks.

2 A: Hi. Can I help you?

C: Can I have a bottle of water, please?

A: Anything else?

C: Yes. A salad.

A: OK. Four dollars, please.

3 A: Can I help you?

C: A tea and a fruit juice, please.

A: Anything else?

C: Yes. Two sandwiches, please.

A: OK. Here you are. Eleven dollars, please.

Unit 5

▶ 75

Look at this fantastic photo. This is a man in the air. His name's Yves Rossy. He's also called the "Jetman"—he can fly. Rossy is from Switzerland. In the photo, Rossy is in the air near mountains in Switzerland. He's in the air for five minutes. It's great!

▶ 77

1 Robots can move.
2 Robots can speak.
3 Robots can carry things.
4 People can't fly.
5 I can speak English.

▶ 79

C = Christine, L = Lewis

L: Hi. Welcome to *Technology Today*. I'm Lewis Jones, and today I'm with Christine Black, a robot expert, and Tomo, a Japanese robot. Hi, Christine.
C: Hi, Lewis.
L: Christine, tell me about this robot.
C: Well, Tomo is from Japan. She's a new kind of robot. She can do things that people can do.
L: "She?" Or "it?"
C: Aha! We say "she." *She's* a robot.
L: OK. So, *she's* from Japan. Can she speak Japanese?
C: Oh, yes, she can speak Japanese and English.
L: OK. Can she sing?
C: Yes, she can.
L: And can she play the piano?
C: Yes, she can.
L: Wow! I can't sing or play the piano. Can she swim?
C: Well, Tomo can't swim, but some robots can swim.
L: OK. Well, my last question is about the name. What does "Tomo" mean?
C: It means "friend" in Japanese.
L: OK, Christine. Thanks very much.
C: Thanks!

▶ 80

a a cat
b a soccer ball
c photos
d a motorcycle
e a watch
f a guitar
g a camera
h glasses

▶ 81

1 I can play the guitar. I have three guitars. This one is interesting. It has a date on it—1921. It's very old.
2 This is our cat. He's named Dylan. He's two years old. He has different colored eyes. One is green and one is blue. He's beautiful.

3 This is my new watch. I like it a lot. Astronauts and pilots wear the same watch. It's very expensive.
4 I have an interesting soccer ball. It's from the 2014 World Cup. It's from a game between Portugal and Germany.

▶ 82

1 I have a bicycle. It's new.
2 My brother has two cameras. They're expensive.
3 My sister has a bag. It's black.
4 My friends have a car. It's small.
5 I have two sisters. They have brown eyes.

▶ 84

a two dollars thirty
b thirteen euros fifty
c fifteen euros
d three euros seventy-five
e seventeen dollars and eighty cents
f eighteen dollars

▶ 85

1 It's thirty dollars.
2 It's forty dollars.
3 It's fifteen dollars.
4 It's sixteen dollars.
5 It's seventy dollars.
6 It's eighteen dollars.

▶ 86

1 **S:** Can I help you?
  C: How much is this alarm clock?
  S: That's a clock radio. It's thirty dollars.
  C: Hmm, that's a bit expensive. Thanks.
  S: That's OK. No problem.
2 **S:** Can I help you?
  C: Yes, I'd like these sunglasses, please.
  S: Certainly.
  C: Oh! Are they for men or women?
  S: They're for men.
  C: That's great.
  S: OK, that's nineteen fifty, please.
  C: Here you are.
3 **C:** Excuse me.
  S: Yes, can I help you?
  C: How much are these memory sticks?
  S: They're five ninety-nine each.
  C: Can I pay with euros?
  S: Yes, of course.

Unit 6

▶ 88

These people love their sports. They aren't players– they're fans. Their

team is called the Kaizer Chiefs. Soccer and rugby are popular sports in South Africa. Soccer is an international sport. About 270 million people play soccer in about 200 countries. The soccer World Cup is every four years. The World Cup prize is millions of dollars—$38 million at the 2018 World Cup in Russia.

▶ 89

1 Running is a sport in the Olympics.
2 Swimming is a sport in water.
3 Cycling is a sport with bicycles.
4 Tennis is a sport with a ball for two or four people.
5 Basketball is a sport with a ball for two teams.

▶ 91

1 I like tennis.
2 I like swimming.
3 I don't like soccer.
4 My friends like sports.
5 I don't like basketball.

▶ 92

Q: Hi. Can I ask you some questions about sports?
A: Yes, of course.
Q: Thanks. Do you like sports?
A: I love sports!
Q: What sports do you like?
A: My favorite sports are tennis and soccer.
Q: Tennis and soccer … thank you.

▶ 93

1 **Q:** Hello. Can I ask you some questions?
  B: OK. What about?
  Q: About sports. Do people in your family like sports?
  B: No, we don't. Well, we only like sports on TV.
  Q: OK. What sports do you like on TV?
  B: Soccer and Formula 1 racing.
2 **Q:** Hi. Can I ask you some questions about sports?
  C: OK.
  Q: Thanks. Do you like basketball?
  C: No, I don't.
  Q: Do you like swimming or cycling?
  C: No, I don't. I don't like sports.
  Q: Oh, OK.

▶ 94

1 Do you like sports?
2 What sports do you like?

▶ 95

Comedies are movies.
Fish are animals.
Wildlife shows are TV shows.

Detective stories are books.
Pop is a type of music.
Scuba diving is a sport.

▶ 97

1 He likes fish.
2 He likes Botswana.
3 He doesn't like cold places.
4 He likes water.
5 He likes coffee.

▶ 98

a fruit
b cheese
c eggs
d meat
e rice
f vegetables

▶ 100

1 A: Let's play ping-pong tomorrow.
  B: No, thanks. I don't like ping-pong.
  A: OK. Let's watch soccer on TV.
  B: I'm sorry. I don't like sports very much. They're boring.
2 C: Let's go to the movie theater this weekend.
  D: That's a good idea. What's on?
  C: A movie with Felicity Jones. It's on at seven o'clock and nine o'clock.
  D: Oh, I love her. She's fantastic.
3 E: Let's have fish tonight.
  F: I'm sorry. I don't like fish. It's horrible.
  E: OK. How about pizza? Do you like pizza?
  F: Pizza's great. Let's invite my sister and her husband.
  E: OK. Send them a text message.

▶ 101

They're boring.
She's fantastic.
It's horrible.
Pizza's great.

Unit 7

▶ 103

The Holi festival—or festival of colors—is in March. It's a very happy festival. It's a celebration of spring and new life. People say "goodbye" to winter and "hello" to spring. In India, the winter months are December, January, and February. The Holi festival is one or two days long. It's a big celebration in parts of India and in other parts of the world.

▶ 105

1 I get up at six o'clock.
2 I have breakfast at six thirty.

3 I start work at seven o'clock.
4 I have lunch in a cafe.
5 I finish work at five forty-five.
6 I have dinner at home.
7 I go to bed at eleven thirty.

▶ 107

I'm Roberto. I'm married and I have two children. I work in an observatory in Chile. I start work at nine o'clock at night. I finish work at 2:30 in the morning and I go home and go to bed. At eight o'clock, I get up and I have breakfast with my wife and children. They go to school at 8:30. They don't go to school on Saturdays and Sundays.

▶ 108

a reading
b cooking
c dancing
d singing
e painting
f walking
g climbing
h shopping

▶ 109

I = interviewer
1 I: Andy, do you have any hobbies?
   A: Yes, I do. My friends and I like to go climbing together. It's exciting!
   I: Do you climb every day?
   A: No, we don't. We climb on Sundays. Our favorite climbing spot is very far away, so we can't climb every day.
2 I: Tina, what are your hobbies?
   T: My hobby is singing. In my free time, I sing in a band with two friends. It's fun. In summer, we go to different towns. I like it.
   I: Do your friends sing?
   T: No, they don't. They play the guitar and the piano.
3 I: Naga, do you have any hobbies?
   N: I don't have many hobbies. I like cooking. I enjoy making food for my family. I cook in the evening. It's nice.
   I: Do you cook for your friends, too?
   N: Yes, I do. They love my food!
4 I: Paul, what are your hobbies?
   P: My hobby is painting. I paint with a group of friends. We meet on Saturdays. We're in a club. It's interesting.
   I: Do you paint pictures of people?
   P: Yes, we do.

▶ 110

1 I: Do you climb every day?
   A: No, we don't. We climb on Sundays.
2 I: Do your friends sing?
   T: No, they don't. They play the guitar and the piano.
3 I: Do you cook for your friends, too?
   N: Yes, I do. They love my food!
4 I: Do you paint pictures of people?
   P: Yes, we do.

▶ 111

1 Do you enjoy shopping?
2 Do you read newspapers?
3 Do your friends go dancing?
4 Do you and your friends play basketball?
5 Do you go climbing?
6 Do you and your friends watch TV?

▶ 113

1 I live in Canada. My favorite time of year is winter. It's cold and snowy.
2 I live in South Africa. I like spring. It's sunny and it isn't cold.
3 I live in the north of Australia. Summer is the wet season. It's hot and rainy. I don't like it!
4 I live in the United States. It's fall here. It's cloudy and it's windy, but I like it.

▶ 115

1 Ooh, I'm cold.
2 I'm tired.
3 I'm thirsty.
4 I'm bored.
5 Mmm, I'm hungry.

▶ 116

M = Mom, D = Dad, P = Paul,
A = Anna
M: What's the matter?
D: It's cold and I'm thirsty.
M: Why don't you have some coffee? Here you are.
D: Thanks. Paul, are you OK?
P: No, I'm not.
M: Why don't you have a sandwich? Here.
P: No, thanks. I'm not hungry. I'm cold and I'm tired.
A: [groans]
M: What's the matter, Anna?
A: I'm bored.
M: Why don't you go swimming?
A: In the rain?!? Mom!
M: I don't understand you all. We're on vacation!

Why don't you have a sandwich?
I don't feel well.
I don't understand you all.

Unit 8

▶ 119

I = interviewer, M = man

I: Do you like your job?

M: Yes, I love my job. I don't work in an office. I work outside. Every day is different in my job.

I: What do you do?

M: I'm a painter. It's an interesting job. I work with a big company. I don't paint houses. I paint ships.

▶ 121

Lily goes to different subway stations. She doesn't drive a train. She's a police officer. Lily walks around train stations. She helps people with problems. Sometimes, she works in a big office. She watches the trains on computer screens.

▶ 122

Naveen enjoys his job.
Lily goes to different subway stations.
She helps people with problems.
Sometimes, she works in a big office.

▶ 124

Q: Why is the school for girls and not boys?

A: In some villages in Kenya, girls don't usually go to school.

Q: Do the girls live at the school?

A: Yes, they do, because it's a long way to their homes and villages.

Q: Does the school have many students?

A: Yes, about two hundred.

Q: Does Kakenya work at the school?

A: Yes, she does.

Q: What does she do?

A: She's the president of the school.

Q: Does she teach?

A: Yes, she does. She sometimes teaches elementary school subjects.

▶ 126

R = receptionist, C = caller

1 R: Good morning. PJ International. Can I help you?

   C: Yes, can I speak to Ed Smith, please?

   R: I'm sorry. He's in a meeting.

   C: OK. Thank you. I'll call back later. Goodbye.

   R: Goodbye.

2 R: Hello. Green Wildlife Park. Can I help you?

   C: Good morning. Can I speak to Mr. Watts, please?

   R: Yes, one moment, please.

   C: Thank you.

3 R: Good morning. City College. Can I help you?

   C: Yes, can I speak to Mrs. Jackson, please?

   R: I'm sorry. She's out of the office at the moment.

   C: OK. Thank you. I'll call back later. Goodbye.

   R: Goodbye.

▶ 127

1 R: Good morning. PJ International. Can I help you?

   C: Yes, can I speak to Ed Smith, please?

   R: I'm sorry. He's in a meeting.

   C: OK. Thank you. I'll call back later. Goodbye.

   R: Goodbye.

3 R: Good morning. City College. Can I help you?

   C: Yes, can I speak to Mrs. Jackson, please?

   R: I'm sorry. She's out of the office at the moment.

   C: OK. Thank you. I'll call back later. Goodbye.

   R: Goodbye.

Unit 9

▶ 130

1 I travel from Singapore to Bangkok for my job. I go every week. I usually go by plane because it's cheap and quick.

2 I'm an Australian student and I travel during my vacations. I love Asia! I travel in Asia by bus. It's really interesting. You meet a lot of people.

3 I live in San Francisco. I often travel to other cities for work. I don't like flying, so I never travel by plane. I usually take the train.

4 I'm from Madrid, but my parents live in Mallorca. I visit them every summer. I usually go by boat.

▶ 133

My suitcase is very small, but that's OK. I only take things I need. My next trip is to Hong Kong. I'm ready to go. So, what's in my suitcase? Well, there's my laptop, of course. And there are two shirts for work. There's a dress for the evening and there's a pair of shoes. And finally, there are some T-shirts and shorts. That's all I need.

▶ 134

There are two shirts.
There are some books.
There are some T-shirts.

▶ 135

1 TV
2 bathtub
3 bed
4 chair
5 lamp
6 desk
7 couch
8 shower
9 fridge

▶ 136

S = Sandra, L = Lucia

S: OK, that's the flight. Now let's look for a hotel. Is it for two nights or three?

L: Three nights—Friday, Saturday, and Sunday. Are there any hotels near the airport?

S: Yes, there are. There are two or three, I think. Oh! This one's expensive!

L: Is there a cheap hotel near the airport?

S: No, there aren't any cheap hotels near the airport.

L: OK. Let's look in the city center. Are there any cheap hotels there?

S: Yes, there are.

L: Well, that's good. Is there a bus to the city center?

S: A bus from the airport? Yes, there is. There's a bus every twenty minutes from the airport to the center. There isn't a train. Is that OK?

L: I think the bus is fine. OK, so let's look at these hotels.

▶ 138

R: Good afternoon. Can I help you?

G1: Hello. I have a reservation for two nights.

R: Of course. Can I have your name, please? And a credit card?

G1: Here you are. My name's on the card.

R: OK. That's fine. Your room is 137.

G1: Thanks. I'd like help with these bags.

R: That's no problem. Just a moment.

G1: And is there a restaurant?

R: Yes, there is. It's open from 7 a.m. to 11 p.m.

G2: Can you tell me the Wi-Fi password?

R: Certainly. It's the name of the hotel—sunhotel. That's one word.

G2: Thanks. And can you call a taxi, please?

R: Yes, of course. Do you want it now?

G2: No, we'd like it for two o'clock.

R: OK.

▶ **139**

I'd like help with these bags.
We'd like it for two o'clock.

Unit 10

▶ **141**

This is a photo of Ayrton Senna, the famous Formula 1 driver. Senna was Brazilian. He was the Formula 1 world champion three times—in 1988, 1990, and 1991. This photo is from 1994. Senna is in Italy. The photo is from just before his last Formula 1 race.

▶ **143**

Albert Einstein lived from 1879 to 1955.
Nelson Mandela lived from 1918 to 2013.
John Lennon lived from 1940 to 1980.
Isabel Allende was born in 1942.
Ayrton Senna lived from 1960 to 1994.
Malala Yousafzai was born in 1997.

▶ **144**

The first around-the-world expedition was from 1519 to 1522. The expedition captain was Ferdinand Magellan.

The first successful South Pole expedition was in 1911. The expedition leader was Roald Amundsen.

The first man in space was Yuri Gagarin. The first woman in space was Valentina Tereshkova. They were both from Russia.

The first woman at the top of Everest was Junko Tabei on May 16th, 1975.

The first woman at the North Pole was Ann Bancroft on May 1st, 1986.

▶ **145**

1 Yuri Gagarin was born in 1934.
2 His parents were farmers.
3 He was a pilot.

▶ **146**

first	eleventh
second	twelfth
third	thirteenth
fourth	fourteenth
fifth	fifteenth
sixth	sixteenth
seventh	seventeenth
eighth	eighteenth
ninth	nineteenth
tenth	twentieth

▶ **147**

May first, 1986
November third, 1957

October fourth, 1957
April twelfth, 1961
December thirteenth, 1972
December fourteenth, 1911
May sixteenth, 1975
July twentieth, 1969

▶ **149**

1 I = interviewer, J = Joe

I: Joe, who was important to you when you were young?

J: Well, I love animals. I remember David Attenborough and his shows about animals.

I: Was he on TV?

J: Yes, he was.

I: Were the shows only for children?

J: No, they weren't. They were for everyone.

I: Can you remember your favorite David Attenborough show?

J: I think it was a show about meerkats. They were really funny! I love animals and science.

2 I = interviewer, A = Aneta

I: Aneta, who was important to you when you were young?

A: Well, I love reading. English was my favorite subject at school. My favorite book was *Frankenstein*.

I: Who was the writer of *Frankenstein*?

A: It was Mary Shelley. She was a very clever woman and a great writer.

I: Were you good at English?

A: Yes, I was.

▶ **150**

I = interviewer, O = Olga

I: Olga, who was important to you when you were young?

O: I remember Michael Johnson. He was a great athlete.

I: Was he an Olympic champion?

O: Yes, he was. Four times. The last time was in 2000.

I: Were the 2000 Olympic Games in Beijing?

O: No, they weren't. They were in Sydney.

I: Were you good at sports in school?

O: No, I wasn't.

▶ **152**

1 T = teacher, S = student

T: Hello, Tom!

S: Hi, Ms. Ross. I'm sorry I'm late. The train was late.

T: That's OK. Take a seat. Turn to page 22.

2 C: Oh. Hi, Ravi.

R: Hi, Clare.

C: Um, the meeting was at 2:30. Where were you?

R: Oh, I'm sorry. I was very busy.

C: It's OK. It wasn't an important meeting.

3 A: Mmm, this coffee is good!

B: Yes, it is.

A: So, where were you yesterday? We were at your house at ten o'clock.

B: I'm very sorry. We weren't at home. We were at my sister's house.

A: It's OK. Don't worry.

▶ **153**

1 I'm sorry I'm late.
2 The train was late.
3 I was very busy.
4 We weren't at home.

Unit 11

▶ **155**

The city of Timbuktu in Mali is famous for its books and documents. Timbuktu was a center of learning for hundreds of years. There were thousands of documents on mathematics, science, art, and other subjects. Many of the books and documents were in libraries and family homes. Some books are four hundred years old.

▶ **157**

The scientists at the University of Innsbruck started their investigation. It was a man. They called him Ötzi because the body was in the Ötztal mountains. The scientists finished their report about Ötzi. He lived about 5,000 years ago. He was a small man. He was about forty-five years old when he died. The scientists think an arrow killed Ötzi.

▶ **159**

1 My friend walked across the Alps in 2016.
2 I started my course last year.
3 Our vacation ended last Sunday.
4 We watched a great movie last week.

▶ **160**

I = Interviewer, D = Dinah

I: Hi, Dinah. New Orleans is very important in your life. Were you born there?

D: Yes, I was.

I: Did you live there when you were a child?

D: Yes, I did. I went to school there, and I studied at college there, too. My father and his grandparents were also born in New Orleans. So the city is very important in my family's history.

I: What did you want to be when you were a child?

D: I wanted to be an artist. My parents are both artists.

I: Did you study art in college?

D: No, actually, I didn't study art! I studied music.

I: Why did you decide to be a musician?

D: Music is part of the story of my city. And now I write songs about the people from my city. They tell me their stories—all about their lives in New Orleans—and I sing about them.

▶ 161

1 Did you study English in school?
2 Did you meet your best friend at school?
3 Did you live in a big city when you were young?
4 Did you start work this year?
5 Did you take a vacation last year?

▶ 163

1 A: Did you and Sonia have a good time in Sydney last week?
   B: Yes, thanks, we did. But we didn't go swimming.
   A: Oh? Why not?
   B: There was a shark in the water!
2 C: Did you and Jack have a good vacation last year?
   D: No, we didn't.
   C: Oh? Why not?
   D: Well, we didn't have any money, so we just stayed at home.
3 E: Did you and Anita have a nice meal last night?
   F: Yes, we did. It was delicious. And we didn't pay!
   E: Oh? Why not?
   F: My boss paid!

▶ 164

1 But we didn't go swimming.
2 Well, we didn't have any money.
3 And we didn't pay!

Unit 12

▶ 166

A: I love the weekend. I get up late and go shopping in town.
B: Oh, I never get up late on weekends. I play soccer on Saturday mornings. We start at eight o'clock.

C: I usually get up late on Saturdays, but not on Sundays. On Sundays, I usually meet friends and we go out for a meal.
A: I go out for meals too, but with my family. We always go to the same place. I love our family lunches!

▶ 167

1 a stove, a fridge   kitchen
2 a chair, a table   dining room
3 an armchair, a couch   living room
4 a bed, a wardrobe   bedroom
5 a bathtub, a shower, a toilet bathroom

▶ 169

Q: Tell us about these photos of Ayu's family.
A: Well, this is Ayu's mother. She's in the kitchen. She's cooking.
Q: What's she making?
A: She's making lunch. They have a big family lunch every Saturday.
Q: And who's this?
A: That's Ayu's husband, Amir. He's bathing their daughter in the bathroom.
Q: How old is their daughter?
A: She's eighteen months old. And this is Ayu's father with his friend. They're talking and drinking coffee.
Q: Are they sitting outside or inside?
A: They're inside. This next photo is Amir's brother with his son.
Q: What are they doing? Are they reading?
A: No, they aren't. They're playing a game on Amir's tablet.
Q: And what about this last one?
A: This is Ayu's brother—he's wearing an orange T-shirt—and his friend. They're washing their motorcycles. They do that every Saturday.
Q: Which is your favorite photo?
A: Oh, I think it's the one of Ayu's husband and daughter, because they are both smiling and happy.

▶ 170

A: What are you doing next weekend?
B: I'm not sure. My brother is coming over tomorrow.
A: Is he staying the weekend?
B: Yes, he is. We're going out for dinner on Saturday evening.
A: Helen Smith is giving a talk on Sunday afternoon. Do you want to come?
B: Yes, that's a great idea.

▶ 171

1 What are you doing this weekend?
2 Are they doing their homework?
3 I'm going shopping.
4 We're going out for dinner.

▶ 173

B = Brad, S = Samira, K = Kris

B: Samira, would you like a drink? A cup of tea or coffee? Kris, what about you?
S: Yes, please. I'd like a cup of tea.
K: Tea for me, too. So, Brad. When are you moving to your new house?
B: On Monday. We're having our last lunch in our old house on Sunday. Would you like to come?
S: OK, sure!
K: Sorry, I can't make it! I'd like to come, but I'm going on vacation on Sunday.
B: Well, do you want to have lunch in our new house next month?
K: That sounds great. Any time after next Saturday is fine.

▶ 174

1 Would you like to come?
2 Would you like to sit down?
3 Would you like a snack?
4 Would you like a drink?

NATIONAL GEOGRAPHIC
L E A R N I N G

Life Student's Book 1, **2nd Edition**
Helen Stephenson, John Hughes, Paul Dummett

Vice President, Editorial Director:
  John McHugh

Publisher: Andrew Robinson

Senior Development Editor: Derek Mackrell

Assistant Editor: Don Clyde Bhasy

Director of Global Marketing: Ian Martin

Senior Product Marketing Manager:
  Caitlin Thomas

Media Researcher: Rebecca Ray,
  Leila Hishmeh

Senior IP Analyst: Alexandra Ricciardi

IP Project Manager: Carissa Poweleit

Senior Director, Production:
  Michael Burggren

Production Manager: Daisy Sosa

Content Project Manager: Beth McNally

Manufacturing Planner:
  Mary Beth Hennebury

Art Director: Brenda Carmichael

Cover Design: Lisa Trager

Text design: emc design ltd.

Compositor: Doubleodesign Ireland, Ltd

American Adaptation: Kasia McNabb

For product information and technology assistance, contact us at
Cengage Learning Customer & Sales Support, cengage.com/contact

For permission to use material from this text or product, submit all requests online at **cengage.com/permissions**
Further permissions questions can be emailed to
permissionrequest@cengage.com

Student Book + App: 978-1-337-90562-6
Student Book + App + My Life Online: 978-1-337-90568-8

National Geographic Learning
20 Channel Center Street
Boston, MA 02210
USA

National Geographic Learning, a Cengage Learning Company, has a mission to bring the world to the classroom and the classroom to life. With our English language programs, students learn about their world by experiencing it. Through our partnerships with National Geographic and TED Talks, they develop the language and skills they need to be successful global citizens and leaders.

Locate your local office at **international.cengage.com/region**

Visit National Geographic Learning online at **NGL.Cengage.com/ELT**
Visit our corporate website at **www.cengage.com**

CREDITS

Text: pp 9–10: recording: David Doubilet; p10: recording Mireya Mayor; p15: source: 'Map "Ring Around N.Y.C."', National Geographic, 2009, page 6; p72: sources: 'Interview with Zeb Hogan', National Geographic Kids, and 'Freshwater Hero: Zeb Hogan', National Geographic; p96: sources: 'Explorer Bio: Kakenya Ntaiya', National Geographic, and 'Video "Kakenya Ntaiya", Educator and Activist', National Geographic; p99: sources: 'Tigers', by Caroline Alexander, National Geographic, December 2011, and 'Africa Vet's "House Calls" Aid Wild Cats, Film Reveals', by Brian Handwerk, National Geographic Ultimate Explorer, January 23, 2004; p111: source: 'Road-Tripping the Trans-Siberian Highway', by McKenzie Funk, National Geographic Adventure, June/July 2008; p130: sources: 'Last Hours of the Iceman', by Stephen Hall, National Geographic, September 2007, 'Iceman Autopsy', by Stephen Hall, National Geographic, November 2011, 'Who killed the Iceman?', National Geographic, February 2000, and https://en.wikipedia. org/wiki/Ötzi; p132: source: 'Explorer Bio: Caroline Gerdes', National Geographic; p135: source: 'Stone Forest', by Neil Shea, National Geographic, November 2009; p147: source: 'Saving Energy Starts at Home', National Geographic, March 2009.
Cover: © Chris Burkard/Massif.
Photos: 6 (tl) © Everett Collection Historical/Alamy Stock Photo; 6 (tr) Mr Standfast/Alamy Stock Photo; 6 (b) Karol Kozlowski/Alamy Stock Photo; 7 (t) © Eric CHRETIEN/Gamma-Rapho/Getty Images; 7 (bl) © Michael Nichols/National Geographic Creative; 7 (br) © Jill Schneider/National Geographic Creative; 8 (tl) © David Doubilet/National Geographic Creative; 8 (tm) imageBROKER/Alamy Stock Photo; 8 (tr) © Medford Taylor/ National Geographic Creative; 8 (mtl) © Gerd Ludwig/National Geographic Creative; 8 (mtm) © Laurent Gillieron/AFP/Getty Images; 8 (mtr) © Lefty Shivambu/Gallo Images/Getty Images; 8 (mbl) © Dibyangshu Sarkar/AFP/Getty Images; 8 (mbm) © Zay Yar Lin; 8 (mbr) © Michael S. Lewis/National Geographic Creative; 8 (bl) © Dario Mitidieri/Getty Images; 8 (bm) © Brent Stirton/Getty Images; 8 (br) © Lynsey Addario/National Geographic Creative; 9 © David Doubilet/National Geographic Creative; 10 (l) © Mauricio Handler/National Geographic Creative; 10 (r) © Mark Thiessen/National Geographic Creative; 11 (tl) © Ryan McVay/Getty Images; 11 (tr) © Westend61 GmbH/Alamy Stock Photo; 11 (ml) © Ozaiachin/Shutterstock.com; 11 (mr) © Fotosoroka/Shutterstock.com; 11 (bl) © Carlos E. Santa Maria/Shutterstock.com; 11 (br) Julia Bellack/Alamy Stock Photo; 12 (t) Andrey Arkusha/ Alamy Stock Photo; 12 (b) Gallo Images/Alamy Stock Photo; 13 (left col: tl) Terry Allen/Alamy Stock Photo; 13 (left col: tr) © Ilya Andriyanov/ Shutterstock.com; 13 (left col: bl) Larry Lilac/Alamy Stock Photo; 13 (left col: br) Blend Images/Alamy Stock Photo; 13 (right col: tl) © Icon Sportswire/ Getty Images; 13 (right col: tr) © Timolina/Shutterstock.com; 13 (right col: m) Iain Masterton/Alamy Stock Photo; 13 (right col: b) © Andrea Pistolesi/ Getty Images; 14 (t) © Corepics VOF/Shutterstock.com; 14 (b) PhotoAlto/Alamy Stock Photo; 15 (t) © CRS PHOTO/Shutterstock.com; 15 (mt) Andres Rodriguez/Alamy Stock Photo; 15 (mb) Custom Medical Stock Photo/Alamy Stock Photo; 15 (b) © LatinStock Collection/Alamy Stock Photo; 16 (tl) ©

Printed in China by CTPS
Print Number: 01 Print Year: 2018

Diego Cervo/Shutterstock.com; 124 (br) © Joel Sartore/National Geographic Creative; 126 © Everett Collection Historical/Alamy Stock Photo; 127 (tl) © iurii/Shutterstock.com; 127 (tr) © Andrey Armyagov/Shutterstock.com; 127 (bl) © Beehive Illustration; 127 (br) © godrick/Shutterstock.com; 128 © Dan Istitene/Getty Images; 129 © Brent Stirton/Getty Images; 131 (l) © South Tyrol Museum of Archaeology/AP/dapd/AP Images; 131 (tr, br) © Kenneth Garrett/National Geographic Creative; 132 (t) © Robert Gilio; 132 (b) © Laura Gerdes Colligan; 135 (all) © Stephen Alvarez/National Geographic Creative; 136 © David Doubilet/National Geographic Creative; 137 Nancy G Stock Photography, Nancy Greifenhagen/Alamy Stock Photo; 138 Derek Phillips/Alamy Stock Photo; 140 © Michael Melford/National Geographic Creative; 141 © Lynsey Addario/National Geographic Creative; 142–143 (all) © Greg Dale/National Geographic Creative; 145 © Yann Layma/Getty Images; 147 (t, b) © Tyrone Turner/National Geographic Creative; 148 J Hayward/Alamy Stock Photo; 149 UpperCut Images/Alamy Stock Photo; 150 Karol Kozlowski/Alamy Stock Photo; 152 © Richard Nowitz/National Geographic Creative; 153 (tl) © Jose Fuste Raga/Getty Images; 153 (tr) © Sven Creutzmann/Getty Images; 153 (b) © Gilbert M. Grosvenor/National Geographic Creative; 155 (l) © Ira Block/National Geographic Creative; 155 (tr) © Sven Creutzmann/Getty Images; 155 (br) © Gilbert M. Grosvenor/National Geographic Creative; 157 (tl) © Nataliia K/Shutterstock.com; 157 (tm) © Dmitry Lobanov/Shutterstock.com; 157 (tr) incamerastock/Alamy Stock Photo; 157 (mtr) Evgeny Karandaev/Alamy Stock Photo; 157 (mtm) © s-ts/Shutterstock.com; 157 (mtr) © Jiraporn Fakchaiyaphum/Shutterstock.com; 157 (mbl) Helen Sessions/Alamy Stock Photo; 157 (mbm) © MaraZe/Shutterstock.com; 157 (mbr) Art Directors & TRIP/Alamy Stock Photo; 157 (b) © Greg Dale/National Geographic Creative; 158 (l) Hero Images Inc./Alamy Stock Photo; 158 (m) Blend Images/Alamy Stock Photo; 158 (r) © Egyptian Studio/Shutterstock.com; 159 (tl) © Nadino/Shutterstock.com; 159 (tr) © Elsa Hoffmann/Shutterstock.com; 159 (ml) © Juanmonino/Getty Images; 159 (mr) © National Geographic Learning; 159 (bl) © VaLiza/Shutterstock.com; 159 (br) Design Pics Inc/Alamy Stock Photo; 176 (tl) © AFP/Getty Images; 176 (tr) Glasshouse Images/Alamy Stock Photo; 176 (b) Pictorial Press Ltd/Alamy Stock Photo.

Illustrations: 6–7 © National Geographic Maps. DATA SOURCES: Shaded relief and bathymetry: GTOPO30, USGS EROS Data Center, 2000. ETOPO1/Amante and Eakins, 2009. Land cover: Natural Earth. naturalearthdata.com. Population Density: LandScan 2012 Global Population Database. Developed by Oak Ridge National Laboratory (ORNL), July 2013. Distributed by East View Geospatial: geospatial.com and East View Information Services: eastview.com/online/landscan. Original copyright year: 2015; 15, 31 (t), 56, 111, 115 (t), 123, 130 David Russell; 19 (r), 24, 31, 43, 48 (l), 55, 67, 79, 81, 83, 91, 114, 115, 139, 151, 160 (right col), 170 Laszlo Veres/Beehive Illustration; 19, 33, 34, 46, 47, 72, 73 (b), 86, 105, 144 Matthew Hams; 21, 41 Martin Sanders/Beehive Illustration; 34 (t) emc design; 48 (r), 73 (t), 82, 88, 165 Alex Hedworth/Eye Candy Illustration; 154, 156, 158, 159, 162, 172, 178 Trystan Mitchell/Beehive Illustration; 160 (left col), 161, 164, 166, 174, 175, 180, 181 Robin Lawrie/Beehive Illustration.

ACKNOWLEDGEMENTS

The *Life* publishing team would like to thank the following teachers and students who provided invaluable and detailed feedback on the first edition:
Armik Adamians, Colombo Americano, Cali; Carlos Alberto Aguirre, Universidad Madero, Puebla; Anabel Aikin, La Escuela Oficial de Idiomas de Coslada, Madrid, Spain; Pamela Alvarez, Colegio Eccleston, Lanús; Manuel Antonio, CEL – Unicamp, São Paolo; Bob Ashcroft, Shonan Koka University; Linda Azzopardi, Clubclass; Éricka Bauchwitz, Universidad Madero, Puebla, Mexico; Paola Biancolini, Università Cattolica del Sacro Cuore, Milan; Lisa Blazevic, Moraine Valley Community College; Laura Bottiglieri, Universidad Nacional de Salta; Richard Brookes, Brookes Talen, Aalsmeer; Alan Broomhead, Approach International Student Center; Maria Cante, Universidad Madero, Puebla; Carmín Castillo, Universidad Madero, Puebla; Ana Laura Chacón, Universidad Madero, Puebla; Somchao Chatnaridom, Suratthani Rajabhat University, Surat Thani; Adrian Cini, British Study Centres, London; Andrew Clarke, Centre of English Studies, Dublin; Mariano Cordoni, Centro Universitario de Idiomas, Buenos Aires; Kevin Coughlan, Westgate Corporation; Monica Cuellar, Universidad La Gran Colombia, Colombia; Jacqui Davis-Bowen, St Giles International; Maria del Vecchio, Nihon University, Nuria Mendoza Dominguez, Universidad Nebrija, Madrid; Robin Duncan, ITC London; Christine Eade, Libera Università Internazionale degli Studi Sociali Guido Carli, Rome; Colegios de Alto Rendimiento, Ministry of Education of Peru; Leopoldo Pinzon Escobar, Universidad Catolica; Joanne Evans, Linguarama, Berlin; Scott Ferry, UC San Diego ELI; Juan David Figueroa, Colombo Americano, Cali; Emmanuel Flores, Universidad del Valle de Puebla; Bridget Flynn, Centro Colombo Americano Medellin; Sally Fryer, University of Sheffield, Sheffield; Antonio David Berbel García, Escuela Oficial de Idiomas de Almería, Spain; Lia Gargioni, Feltrinelli Secondary School, Milan; Roberta Giugni, Galileo Galilei Secondary School, Legnano; Monica Gomez, Universidad Pontificia Bolivariana; Doctor Erwin Gonzales, Centro de Idiomas Universidad Nacional San Agustin, Peru; Ivonne Gonzalez, Universidad de La Sabana; J Gouman, Pieter Zandt Scholengemeenschap, Kampen; Cherryll Harrison, UNINT, Rome; Lottie Harrison, International House Recoleta; Marjo Heij, CSG Prins Maurits, Middelharnis; María del Pilar Hernández, Universidad Madero, Puebla; Luz Stella Hernandez, Universidad de La Sabana, Colombia; Rogelio Herrera, Colombo Americano, Cali; Amy Huang, Language Canada, Taipei; Huang Huei-Jiun, Pu Tai Senior High School; Carol Humme, Moraine Valley Community College; Nelson Jaramillo, Colombo Americano, Cali; Jacek Kaczmarek, Xiehe YouDe High School, Taipei; Thurgadevi Kalay, Kaplan, Singapore; Noreen Kane, Centre of English Studies, Dublin; Billy Kao, Jinwen University of Science and Technology; Shih-Fan Kao, Jinwen University of Science and Technology, Taipei; Youmay Kao, Mackay Junior College of Medicine, Nursing, and Management, Taipei; Fleur Kelder, Vechtstede College, Weesp; Waseem Khan, YBM; Dr Sarinya Khattiya, Chiang Mai University; Lucy Khoo, Kaplan; Karen Koh, Kaplan, Singapore; Susan Langerfeld, Liceo Scientifico Statale Augusto Righi, Rome; Hilary Lawler, Centre of English Studies, Dublin; Jon Leachtenauer, Ritsumeikan University; Eva Lendi, Kantonsschule Zürich Nord, Zürich; Michael Ryan Lesser, Busan University of Foreign Studies; Evon Lo, Jinwen University of Science and Technology; Peter Loftus, Centre of English Studies, Dublin; José Luiz, Inglês com Tecnologia, Cruzeiro; Christopher MacGuire, UC Language Center, Chile; Eric Maher, Centre of English Studies, Dublin; Nick Malewski, ITC London; Claudia Maribell Loo, Universidad Madero, Puebla; Malcolm Marr, ITC London; Graciela Martin, ICANA (Belgrano); Michael McCollister, Feng Chia University; Erik Meek, CS Vincent van Gogh, Assen; Marlene Merkt, Kantonsschule Zürich Nord, Zürich; Jason Montgomery, YBM; David Moran, Qatar University, Doha; Rosella Morini, Feltrinelli Secondary School, Milan; Christopher Mulligan, Ritsumeikan University; Judith Mundell, Quarenghi Adult Learning Centre, Milan; Cinthya Nestor, Universidad Madero, Puebla; Nguyen Dang Lang, Duong Minh Language School; Peter O'Connor, Musashino University, Tokyo; Cliona O'Neill, Trinity School, Rome; María José Colón Orellana, Escola Oficial d'Idiomes de Terrassa, Barcelona; Viviana Ortega, Universidad Mayor, Santiago; Luc Peeters, Kyoto Sangyo University, Kyoto; Sanja Brekalo Pelin, La Escuela Oficial de Idiomas de Coslada, Madrid; Itzel Carolina Pérez, Universidad Madero, Puebla, Mexico; Sutthima Peung, Rajamangala University of Technology Rattanakosin; Marina Pezzuoli, Liceo Scientifico Amedeo Avogadro, Rome; Andrew Pharis, Aichi Gakuin University, Nagoya; Hugh Podmore, St Giles International, UK; Carolina Porras, Universidad de La Sabana; Brigit Portilla, Colombo Americano, Cali; Soudaben Pradeep, Kaplan; Judith Puertas, Colombo Americano, Cali; Takako Ramsden, Kyoto Sangyo University, Kyoto; Sophie Rebel-Dijkstra, Aeres Hogeschool; Zita Reszler, Nottingham Language Academy, Nottingham; Sophia Rizzo, St Giles International; Gloria Stella Quintero Riveros, Universidad Catolica; Cecilia Rosas, Euroidiomas; Eleonora Salas, IICANA Centro, Córdoba; Victoria Samaniego, La Escuela Oficial de Idiomas de Pozuelo de Alarcón, Madrid; Jeanette Sandre, Universidad Madero, Puebla; Bruno Scafati, ARICANA; Anya Shaw, International House Belgrano, Argentina; Anne Smith, UNINT, Rome & University of Rome Tor Vergata, Italy; Courtney Smith, US Ling Institute; Suzannah Spencer-George, British Study Centres, Bournemouth; Students of Cultura Inglesa, São Paulo; Makiko Takeda, Aichi Gakuin University, Nagoya; Jilly Taylor, British Study Centres, London; Caroline S. Tornatore, Austin Community College; Juliana Trisno, Kaplan, Singapore; Ruey Miin Tsao, National Cheng Kung University, Tainan City; Michelle Uitterhoeve, Vechtstede College, Weesp; Anna Maria Usai, Liceo Spallanzani, Rome; Carolina Valdiri, Colombo Americano, Cali, Colombia; Keith Vargo, Westgate Corporation; Gina Vasquez, Colombo Americano, Cali; Andreas Vikran, NET School of English, Milan; Helen Ward, Oxford, UK; Mimi Watts, Università Cattolica del Sacro Cuore, Milan; Yvonne Wee, Kaplan Higher Education Academy; Christopher Wood, Meijo University; Kevin Wu, Hangzhou No.14 High School; Yanina Zagarrio, ARICANA.